To
MARY Ruth
All My Best

Ludlow Porch

2-1-86

There's Nothing Neat About Seeing Your Feet

The life & times of a fat American

LUDLOW PORCH

PEACHTREE PUBLISHERS, LIMITED

Published by
PEACHTREE PUBLISHERS, LTD.
494 Armour Circle, N.E.
Atlanta, Georgia 30324

Manufactured in the United States of America

First printing

Library of Congress Catalog Number 84-60923

ISBN: 0-931948-65-7

This book is dedicated to the memory of
Frank Gordy, founder of my beloved Varsity.

Special thanks go to Jean Hendrix, the Downtown YMCA, the Dictaphone Corporation, and to the fat people of the world, without whose help the writing of this book would not have been necessary.

Foreword

I ALWAYS HAD a sense of humor about my weight problem. Others around me didn't.

I spent a large part of my life trying to convince them that life without humor is like fresh peach pie without homemade whipped cream. I enjoy making people laugh; so does my friend Ludlow Porch.

If you would sell your sister for a good piece of fried chicken ... if you ever laid down on your bedroom floor and attempted to zip up your pants ... if the M&M you found in the couch began looking good to you ... then *There's Nothing Neat About Seeing Your Feet* should be part of your library.

You will laugh yourself thin, I promise.

— Richard Simmons

Books by Ludlow Porch

A View from the Porch

The Cornbread Chronicles

Contents

Part I

GETTING THERE

1

Even Dorothy Lamour Had Ugly Feet

I WAS SUCH a skinny kid that my mother worried constantly about my weight. I was skinnier than a clothesline. "You look *pore*," my mother used to say. "The neighbors will think we're not feeding you." So she set out to quieten the neighbors and fatten me.

She spooned mounds of sugar on my oatmeal every morning ("Oatmeal sticks to your ribs," she said) and heaped my plate with potatoes at dinner and biscuits and gravy at supper. I washed it all down with gallons of Ovaltine. And there was no end to the pies and cakes and cobblers she made for dessert in hopes of fattening me up.

But nothing seemed to work. I was still so skinny that my belt wouldn't hold my pants up, and I was forced into the indignity of wearing suspenders. Do you know how it feels to be the only kid in the fifth grade wearing suspenders? I didn't know a lot about fashion in those days, but I did know that Hopalong Cassidy didn't wear suspenders. Even Gabby Hayes, one of the worse dressed cowboys of all, didn't wear suspenders.

I was humiliated and too embarrassed to look any of my classmates in the eyes. Consequently, I spent a lot of time staring at my feet. I soon discovered that there's nothing uglier in this world than feet, and no amount of toenail polish or pedicures or foot lotions can change that.

Since the beginning of time, there's never been a pair of pretty feet. Cleopatra's pet snake bit her on the foot because he thought her toes were rivals.

Remember Dorothy Lamour, the beautiful movie star? She had jet black hair framing a face that was prettier than a fifty-dollar pocket knife, and her body was almost perfect. Almost.

Consider this: Did you ever see a close-up of Dorothy Lamour's feet? Never. Like everybody else, even the Sarong Girl had ugly feet.

Years later I caught a glimpse of Marilyn Monroe's feet in a movie and thought maybe I'd found my first pair of pretty feet. Then I looked closer and saw little black hairs sticking out of her great toes. It was enough to turn a possum's stomach.

So there I was in the fifth grade — embarrassed by my suspenders and grossed out by the sight of my own feet. I came to hate my feet. Ugly, misshapen blobs! I swore that one day I'd gain enough weight that I wouldn't have to wear suspenders to hold up my pants, and I wouldn't be embarrassed and have to stare at my feet.

My plan eventually worked. I gained so much weight that I didn't have to wear suspenders or look at my feet. My pants were tighter than tree bark, and I couldn't see my feet for my protruding stomach. That's all right, I thought; there's nothing neat about seeing your feet. I considered all the many advantages of being fat:

—Neighbors won't say that your mama isn't feeding you.

—You get more for your money when you buy belts.

—You become very proficient at math by figuring the load limits of bridges.

—You supply shade for small animals.

—You don't need a cushion at Little League games.

—You never have to drink Tab. Ever.

—You don't sweat; you render.

—If there's a famine, you'll live longer than the joggers.

Then I made a list of the disadvantages of being fat. The list was longer than a Presbyterian sermon. I realized for the first time that there are things in life worse than wearing suspenders.

Since that time, I have spent most of my adult life trying to get another look at my feet. This is the story of that quest.

15

'Anyone who eats three
meals a day should
understand why
cookbooks outsell sex
books three to one.'

— *L. M. Boyd*

2

Was My Father Really a Water Buffalo?

THERE IS PROBABLY no one reason that explains why some of us tend to double our weight every two meals while our more fortunate brothers and sisters can eat with both hands and still wear designer jeans. Over the years, I have tried every way possible to rationalize my fatness — perhaps to ease the mental pain of knowing that I have the willpower of a wino.

I once told my doctor that I thought I was overweight because of my glands. He said there was no case in recorded medical history where a man had two-hundred-pound glands. I hate snotty doctors.

Then I suggested to this same physician that my problem was hereditary. "I feel that's highly unlikely," he said, "unless you happen to be the offspring of two love-crazed water buffaloes."

Not being one who discourages easily, I said, "Well, Doc, maybe I just don't get enough exercise."

He said that if I didn't cut back on my eating, a daily jog to Scandinavia wouldn't help. Like I said, I hate snotty doctors.

There are many other rationalizations, and I've tried them all. Some people use food as a tranquilizer; something goes amiss in their lives and they take it out on a coconut cake. Others eat for something to do with their hands; how many times have you sat watching television and suddenly realized that you've just finished off a twenty-five-pound bag of potato chips? Some people eat because they're bored or happy or have too much energy; still others eat because they're excited or unhappy or don't have enough energy.

But whatever the rationalization, the result is always the same: overweight. And once we cut through all the excuses, the real reason for our condition is that we simply eat too much of the wrong foods. It grieves me to say it, dear hearts, but I'm afraid it's true.

The best explanation I ever heard came from my friend Dennis's doctor. Dennis, who is five-nine and weighs about two hundred and thirty pounds, asked his doctor why he was so fat. "The answer is very simple," said his snotty doctor. "You're eating enough for two men, but the Good Lord blessed you with only one rectum."

The ultimate truism for us tubbos is that fat is often like good luggage — you keep it forever. That doesn't mean we have to stay fat; it just means that we have to be forever aware of what we're stuffing into that disposal below our noses.

My own particular downfall was bread. I honestly believe that if I had been born three thousand years ago, I would have rejected the sun god as a silly superstition and instead would have become the leader of a cult that worshipped bread.

In addition to bread, I also love potatoes. But even that could be an understatement. The truth of the matter is that I place potatoes on a pedestal right up there beside motherhood, Waylon Jennings, and the Magna Carta. Potatoes are the only vegetable I know of that can be eaten three meals a day, seven days a week.

I enjoy butter, too, mainly because it goes so well with bread and potatoes. It also is delicious on all types of vegetables, and if you're on a real eating binge, butter can be eaten like ice cream.

Yes sir, the willpower of a wino.

'A starved body has a
skinny soul.'

— *Marlon Brando*

3

A Shortcut to Strawberry Shortcake

THE FEEDERS OF the world are a fatso's biggest enemy. Feeders, of course, are the folks who associate food with good friends, laughter, and most of all, love. They think that any natural show of hospitality must include something — anything — to eat.

Now, don't get me wrong; I love the feeders. In fact, my mother was one of the great feeders of all time. I used to stop by her house after lunch, and the conversation would go something like this:

"Have you had lunch?"

"Yes ma'am, about thirty minutes ago."

"Did you get enough?"

"Oh, yes ma'am, I'm about to bust."

"I've got some cube steak in the refrigerator. Wouldn't be any trouble to fix you a couple of steak sandwiches."

"No thanks, I'm trying to lose a little weight."

"I could leave the mayonnaise off."

"No, but thanks anyway."

"Do you feel all right?"

"Yes ma'am, I feel fine. I'm just not hungry."

"You used to like to my cube steak sandwiches."

"Mama, I love your cube steak sandwiches."

"Good. How many do you want?"

"Just one, Mama. Just one."

My daughter Barbara was about fifteen when we went on the Weight Watchers' Diet together. Barbara was determined to lose weight, and during the two months she had been on the diet, not one mouthful that was not prescribed had passed her lips. I had been a little less successful, but I was still trying.

One Sunday we went to visit her granny and grand-daddy, who owned a dairy farm in Bostwick, Georgia. This was to be a real test, for there has never been a Southern cook anywhere who could top Barbara's granny. Was it possible to stay on our diet at this wonderful woman's table?

During the meal we did fine, but we could tell that our hostess was not real comfortable with our picky eating. Finally she turned to Barbara and said, "How about a big bowl of strawberry shortcake with whipped cream fresh from the dairy barn?"

"No thanks, Granny," Barbara said. "I'm on a diet."

"Why, child, that can't hurt you. It's pure cream."
Now, that's a hard-core feeder.

My wife Diane is what I call a subtle feeder. She periodically asks, "What can I get you?" And no matter what I answer, she gets it for me.

She is even more subtle than that at mealtime. You see, Diane is the most wonderful cook in the world. Did you ever try eating just a little bit of Beef Wellington or only a small helping of Eggs Benedict?

Of course, feeders aren't the only ones who can destroy a diet. Eaters can do the same; they not only encourage you to eat but also show you how.

The late Lewis Grizzard, Sr., was one of the all-time great eaters. Some of the happiest hours of my life were spent with Lewis, Sr., and more often than not there was a table between us loaded with good things to eat.

Lewis, Sr., and I would be watching a late show on television, and out of the clear blue sky he would say, "Well, Luddy, how about a twelve o'clock snack?" I was easy. The next thing I knew, we were eating fried red hot sandwiches and drinking buttermilk.

He also used to take great delight in coaxing me to go with him to one of those all-you-can-eat places. First Lewis, Sr., would verify with the manager that he could, indeed, have all the chicken or babecue or whatever that he wanted. Then he would encourage me to match him bite for bite, mouthful for mouthful, while two waitresses were kept busy carrying food.

We could see the manager crying over in the corner, mulling over his financial ruin.

One afternoon Lewis, Sr., took me to a fast-food hamburger joint. I didn't want to go with him, but he hated to eat alone. Besides that, he told me that if I didn't go with him, Jesus wouldn't love me anymore. I had enough trouble already, so I agreed to go.

The place was running a special on its great hamburgers, and there was a long line at the window. The man at the front of the line was about six-foot-two and weighed about a hundred and thirty pounds.

Lewis, Sr., walked up and tapped him on the shoulder and said, "Hey there, little fellow. My name is Major Grizzard. Why don't you get behind me and let a man who knows something about eating in the front of this line?" The man was so shocked that he actually moved aside.

Feeders and eaters — you gotta love 'em, but you got to watch 'em.

'A gourmet who thinks of calories is like a tart who looks at her watch.'

— *James Beard*

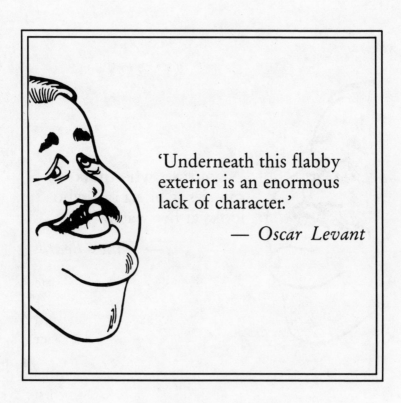

'Underneath this flabby
exterior is an enormous
lack of character.'

— *Oscar Levant*

4

I Scream,
You Scream,
We All Scream ...

IT WOULD BE interesting to find out how many
overweight people in the United States don't like ice
cream. My guess is that it would be zero minus four. I
suspect all are like me: They love the taste and flavors
of ice cream, but eating it is also like a trip down
memory lane.

When I was a small boy, ice cream was the ultimate
treat. I never dreamed about owning a pony or danc-
ing with a tight-sweatered cheerleader. I dreamed
about my next Hunky (that's an Eskimo Pie, for our
Northern readers).

I remember vividly how the alarm would be
sounded. It was the obligation and duty of the first
child who spotted the Hunky Man to alert the neighborhood of his presence. This was done by screaming
at the top of your lungs, "HUNKY MAN!" The cry
would be picked up by your young friends, and

immediately every child in earshot was looking or begging for a nickel.

The more prudent youngsters had advance stashes of nickels and therefore did not have to waste precious seconds explaining to their mamas that "one little Hunky won't hurt my supper."

Once you reached the Hunky Man, you found him surrounded by every child you ever knew. A crowd four or five deep would circle around the white push-cart that was filled with dry ice and various ice cream treats.

The kids who had been unable to come up with a nickel always hung around hoping to talk their best friends into just one lick. One sure-fire method for discouraging these whiners was to spit on your ice cream.

It was the middle-class kids who were always eating the five-cent Hunkies. Rich children, on the other hand, could afford a dime Dreamsicle. I was thirty years old before I tried a Dreamsicle. On the rare occasions when I had a dime, I felt it made more sense to buy two Hunkies than one Dreamsicle.

The girls in the neighborhood always bought a cup of ice cream because it had a picture of a movie star inside on the cardboard lid. All they had to do was lick the ice cream off the lid and there was a picture of Shirley Temple, Lon McAlister, or, if you got lucky, maybe even George Brent.

Hunkies, however, had their surprises, too. If you

found a star under the ice cream on your Hunky stick, you won a free one.

Secretly I always suspected that the Hunky Man was heavily involved in organized crime. You see, I must have eaten well over ten thousand Hunkies in my day, and I never found a star or knew anybody who did. It grieves me to think it, but this scam obviously was the work of the Mafia.

Ice cream has always been an important part of my life. One of the best jobs I ever had was as a soda jerk. It was such a good job, in fact, that I had to serve an apprenticeship to get it.

The apprenticeship had nothing to do with jerking sodas. The only time the apprentice went behind the counter was to shave ice. This was a tough job, accomplished by putting a fifty-pound block of ice in a washtub and cutting it into small pieces with a four-pronged ice shaver.

All other times, the main job of the apprentice was delivering prescriptions on a bicycle. I spent ninety percent of my time peddling and ten percent praying that the soda jerk would die so I could take his job.

When I was finally made a full-time soda jerk, one of the things that thrilled me most was the uniform. It consisted of a white apron that went from waist to shoes, and a snow-white, heavily starched jacket. This magnificent ensemble was topped off by a white, starched garrison cap and a black leather bow tie.

My fame as a soda jerk soon spread. Not only did I look as sharp as a King Hardware pocket knife, but I also took great pride in the wonders that I created behind that beautiful marble counter.

I still remember the formula for my perfect fountain Cokes: a glass full to the brim with shaved ice, one and a half squirts of Coca-Cola syrup, topped off with carbonated water. The secret was in the syrup. The perfect fountain Coke had to have exactly one and a half squirts of syrup.

My real forte was the now-famous Ludlow Luscious Banana Split. This was made by carefully slicing a banana lengthwise and putting it on each side of an oblong glass dish. In the middle of the dish I placed three scoops of ice cream — one vanilla, one chocolate, and one strawberry. These were then generously covered with strawberries, pineapple, and nuts. The entire masterpiece was finally topped off with whipped cream and a cherry.

Once properly prepared, the Ludlow Luscious Banana Split was a meal in itself. This gourmet delight cost twenty-five cents, but I can assure you it was worth every penny.

If you're wondering why you haven't been able to get a good banana split in recent years, allow me to offer my theory about the unfortunate demise of this American delicacy.

In the first place, soda jerks no longer wear the

proper uniform. How can we possibly expect a decent banana split from someone not wearing a black leather bow tie? They also don't wear the starched, white garrison caps anymore. I think long hair forced that change. (I'm sure you remember that period when most teen-aged boys looked like chrysanthemums.)

In the second place, banana splits are no longer served properly. Styrofoam containers and plastic spoons are outrageous. To get the full taste of every mouthful, it is absolutely mandatory that banana splits be eaten out of a glass container with a metal spoon.

It grieves me deeply to think that a full generation has come along without knowing the ecstasy involved in eating a banana split worthy of its name.

The history of ice cream is long and glorious. No one is exactly sure how long this fattening delicacy has been around, but there is evidence that three thousand years ago the Chinese were mixing snow with fruit juice.

In 1295, Marco Polo brought ice cream recipes back to Venice from Peking. And by 1700, ice cream had become a popular dessert among rich American colonists.

Records show that during the summer of 1790, George Washington spent more than two hundred dollars with a New York ice cream merchant. That may not sound like a lot of money today, but it becomes a monstrous amount when you realize that in 1790 land could be bought for ten cents an acre. Twenty years later, Dolly Madison was serving ice cream at the White House.

On a bright summer day in 1846, a breakthrough occurred that would change the course of history for ice cream eaters. It was on that day that Nancy Johnson invented the hand-cranked freezer.

In my opinion, there should be monuments in honor of this great woman. There should be highways, parks, and cities named for her. There should be a Nancy Johnson golf tournament, a Nancy Johnson First Baptist Church, and at least one Willie Nelson album bearing her name.

Without her invention, countless meetings with dinner on the grounds would have been disappointing. Without her I wouldn't have known Uncle Chuck's homemade peach ice cream, and millions of kids wouldn't know the thrill of licking a dasher.

History may have forgotten her, but I never will. On behalf of all children and all fat folks of the world, I say to Nancy Johnson, inventor of the hand-turned ice cream freezer, "Thanks for the memories."

'Middle age is when the narrow waist and the broad mind change places.'
— *Unknown*

'Religions change; beer
and wine remain.'

— *Harvey Allen*

5

Praise the Lord
For Crispy Chicken

LIKE MOST FAT folks, there have been times in my life when I have regarded eating as almost a religious experience. But that's really not so unusual, because like many Southerners, some of my earliest memories are of eating in church.

I attended Sunday school and church regularly in those days — not because I was afraid of the wrath of the Lord, but because I was afraid of the wrath of my mother. Once I was there, the treats made it enjoyable.

When I was in the preschool Sunday school class at the Presbyterian church, the lovely lady who taught the class would always bring us cookies. That was her way of controlling us, and it worked like a charm. Who wouldn't sit quietly for homemade cookies?

Another highlight of those days was when the Sunday school teacher would serve Welch's Grape Juice. I had no idea what it cost, but I knew it was so expensive that we rarely had it at home, and I knew it tasted better with cookies than an R.C. Cola.

Later I noticed that the only time I heard folks pray aloud outside of church was at the table. No matter whose house we went to for dinner, there was always a blessing. My favorite blessing was the short, simple, wonderful one that Terrell Jackson's father used: "Thank the Lord for dinner." And then we dug in.

On the other hand, when the preacher came to our house for dinner, he would always pray till the cornbread was too cold to melt butter.

One Sunday we had a seminary student over for dinner. He must have been really caught up in the spirit, because his blessing was so long that the lettuce in my pear salad turned brown.

I don't know what became of him, but the possibility that he finished school and became a full-time preacher worried me a lot. I always wondered how many folks in his congregation died from salmonella over the years. In the back of my mind, I always regarded him as a sort of Presbyterian Jack the Ripper.

But neither preachers nor seminary students can match Baptist deacons when it comes to returning thanks. They're more full of wind than an Oklahoma tornado.

They don't seem to think it's enough just to be thankful for the meal. They go on to thank the farmer who spent so much time and energy raising the turnip greens. They thank the Lord for the cook. They even give thanks for the cow, who labored long and hard so we could have the butter. Then they thank the Lord for the folks who delivered the chicken feed so we could partake of the wonderful fried chicken, and they thank the kind people who took time out of their busy schedules to wring the chickens' necks. They usually close (mercifully) by calling down God's blessings on the people who made the stove.

Children deliver some of the most creative blessings. Once when I was about thirteen, I spent the night with my friend Buck. We sat down at the dinner table and his mother said, "Return thanks, Buck."

Buck bowed his head and said, "God made the earth and sky so sunny, but wouldn't you know it, He made the gravy too runny." Buck's mama hit him with a bottle of Log Cabin syrup. It must have been a very religious experience for Buck, 'cause the whole time he was trying to stop his nose from bleeding he was hollering, "Oh God! Oh God!"

Looking back over the years, I have very fond memories of our church quarterly meetings. Actually, I wasn't all that wild about the meetings, but I was crazy about the all-day singing and dinner on the grounds.

Folks came to the quarterly meeting from all over the country, and all the women brought a covered dish. It was not uncommon to see a table fifty feet long covered with every wonderful dish known to Southern mankind.

The meats included ham, fried chicken, roast, meatloaf, and barbecue. The vegetables seemed endless: creamed corn, mashed potatoes, potato salad, greens, corn on the cob, squash fixed eighteen different ways, pole beans, butter beans, English peas, and thirty or forty others I frequently dream about.

And for dessert there were always fifteen or twenty cakes and a dozen or so pies. My favorite dessert was the banana pudding, and when that gave out I was partial to the blackberry cobbler.

Sitting on the ground at the end of the table was a No. 3 washtub full of iced tea. The thing that made the tea special was the chunks of ice floating in it. They had been broken up out of a fifty-pound block of ice with an honest-to-goodness ice pick. I don't know exactly why that made such a difference to the taste of the tea, but it certainly did.

We usually arrived at church by eleven o'clock on the days of the quarterly meetings. We'd go right in for a brief service, sing the first and last verses of "How Great Thou Art," and then race outside for dinner.

Everybody would go through the line about twice, and when we'd eaten enough to kill a Poland China hog, we'd sit around in the shade picking our teeth and saying things like, "Wasn't that a good batch of tater salad Miss Sarah brought this year?"

Someone else would add, "Yeh, Lawdie, and don't nobody on earth fry chicken like ole Herbert's widow."

Then somebody else would say, "Did you get any of ole Sam's barbecue?" And the answer invariably would be, "Boy, howdy, did I! He can turn a hog every which way but loose."

After everybody's dinner had settled, we would break up into age groups. The grown-ups would go inside the church and sing hymns for awhile, and then they'd listen to three or four gospel quartets who had been invited for the day. The old men dozed a lot.

The children, meanwhile, either played tag or searched through the bushes and woods for teen-agers. It was always great fun to catch a teen-aged boy trying to steal a kiss from his girl.

When we spotted them, it was part of the ritual to yell, "I'm gonna tell!" The girl would squeal, and the boy would shout, "I'm gonna kill you, you little turd!"

While all this was going on, some of the ladies would be covering the remaining food with table-cloths. This was done so that along about dark, everybody could come and have another crack at the leftovers.

As a veteran of many dinners on the grounds, I have

become something of an expert on denominational cooking. I can actually taste the food and tell you the religious persuasion of the cook. It's really not all that hard; it just requires a little common sense and years of overeating at quarterly meetings.

For example, if you want truly delicious string beans, you must go to a Methodist dinner on the grounds. Green beans properly prepared are cooked almost to pieces; overcooking is the secret to their wonderfulness. Methodists also lead the pack when it comes to fresh creamed corn. There are many ways to fix creamed corn, but those lovely Methodist ladies do it just right — it's thick, creamy, and each and every mouthful is a preview of what Paradise must be like.

On the other hand, if you want fried chicken the way God intended for it to be cooked, you must have it prepared by a Baptist. Theirs always has a thick, golden brown crust on the outside, and it's almost heaven on the inside. Baptist fried chicken will never disappoint you.

Church of Christ members tend to serve delicious cornbread, while Presbyterians specialize in light, flavorful rolls. If your taste runs to something spicy, then Catholic cooking is probably for you. If there's a better way to get heartburn, I haven't found it yet.

Episcopalians do wonders with hams and roasts, but when it comes to lamb and desserts, go to a Greek dinner on the grounds. If butter beans and lima beans are among your favorites, try those prepared by a member of the Church of the Nazarene. The way these folks prepare beans, you'd think they invented them.

One thing that all these denominations have in common is that they serve sweet tea, and so it should be. Anyone who would serve unsweetened tea is not living at the foot of the cross and would be well advised to get right with the Lord.

In retrospect, I suspect that much of the overeating I've done in my life can be traced to those happy times on the church grounds. From those early days with the cookies through the fifty-foot table loaded with food, the pattern was set.

But as much as I hate being obese, I'm not sure I would trade those wonderful, calorie-laden memories for a thin body.

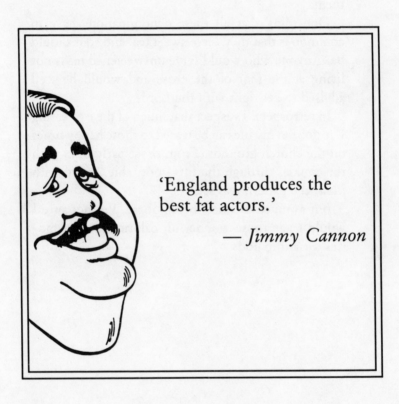

'England produces the
best fat actors.'

— *Jimmy Cannon*

6

Walnettos Were
The Main Attraction

IF YOU'RE A masochist looking for a thrill, or if for
some foul reason you want to test your willpower, try
going to a movie and not eating anything. Movies just
lend themselves to snacking, and I suspect they've
broken more diets than hearts.

The people who handle movie concessions know
what you want, and they make every effort to give it
to you. It's not uncommon to spend as much at the
concession stand as you do at the box office.

Everything is also larger at movie concession
stands. When you buy a Reese's Peanut Butter Cup in
a grocery store, it's good for about two bites. But the
two-pound size they sell at the movies is filled with
enough peanut butter to derail a freight train. And the
last time I bought a tub of popcorn at the movies, I
had to take two seats — one for me and one for the
popcorn.

Ludlow Porch

Snacking at the movies, like eating at the church, occupies a special spot in my memory. It's hard for me to look back and imagine what I might have been like without concession stand calories.

Children in my day took a large measure of pride in their favorite movie candy. We used to brag about our selection and try to get our buddies to try our particular favorite. It also was a popular pastime to ridicule the choice of a less discerning playmate. We'd say things like, "There's ole dumb-ass Rufus. He ain't got no sense. He's eating *pink* B.B. Bats!"

I can still remember all of my friends' favorites. Goforth Wilson's was Mr. Goodbars. Goforth said he enjoyed them because he liked both the milk chocolate and the peanuts. We all enjoyed seeing how messy he could get eating a completely unwrapped Goodbar throughout a double feature.

During the first movie, he would eat the candy bar itself. During the second feature, he would lick the paper and his fingers. Goforth liked to get his money's worth.

My friend Pig liked JuJu Bees — not so much for the taste as for the recreational opportunities they afforded. Pig liked to fill his mouth with JuJu Bees, get them good and slick, and blow them out between his lips onto smaller children. Pig had many of the same personality traits which we have since come to associate with Nazi concentration camp guards.

Skip Grizzard (a.k.a. Lewis, Jr., but he was Skip in those days) was very creative in his movie munching. He would buy Milk Duds and a box of popcorn, chew up a mouthful of Milk Duds, and then pop a handful of popcorn into his mouth. The result was chocolate-and-caramel-covered corn. It was a disgusting thing to do but probably was pretty tasty.

Snake Burnett, the meanest kid who ever walked, never bought candy. He would just prowl up and down the aisle until he saw a smaller kid eating something that struck his fancy. Then Snake would take the little kid's candy. Not even spitting on it would deter Snake.

On one occasion when a well-meaning usher tried to intervene, Snake not only took the kid's candy but also took the usher's flashlight. Snake was not one to be denied his pleasures.

My favorite movie candy was Walnettos. For me, they were perfect. First of all, they cost only a nickel, and it was a rare day indeed when I had more than a nickel to spend at the movies.

Secondly, they tasted like a walnut-flavored chocolate bar — two flavors that I love until this day.

And thirdly, and most importantly, they had staying power. A nickel box of Walnettos would last through a Bob Steel western, a Charlie Chan picture, a Three Stooges comedy, a Tom and Jerry cartoon, and the Movietone news. If I was really resourceful, I could even save one to eat while I peddled my bicycle home.

Norman was the sissy of our age group, and like all sissies he ate Raisinettes at the movies. Norman would finish his Raisinettes during the first picture, go into the bathroom to wash his hands, and come out drying them off on the handkerchief his mother made him carry.

One day I asked him, "Hey, Norman, why don't you dry your hands on paper towels and save your handkerchief for blowing your nose?"

He rolled his beady little eyes toward the ceiling, looked down his sissy nose at me, and said, "Don't be vulgar."

I hit Norman right in the nose — not because he called me vulgar, but because he ate Raisinettes. Now, that's vulgar.

Several years later I went with my parents on a vacation to Florida. One afternoon we went to a movie and I discovered something else vulgar. They were selling cotton candy at the movie concession stand.

I could hardly keep my mind on the movie for watching kids eat cotton candy. I kept thinking they were eating attic insulation.

Through the years I have broken many diets while attending movies. The faint aroma of fresh popcorn mixed with the distant yet audible popping sounds are too much temptation for me to bear. And if the pop-corn doesn't get me, then the memory of Walnettos invariably will.

Diets and movies just don't mix.

'I've known what it is to be hungry, but I always went right to a restaurant.'

— *Ring Lardner*

7

Savor the Flavor
From East to West

WE'VE ALREADY ESTABLISHED that feeders, eaters, ice cream, churches, and movies are bad for diets, but they're bush league problems compared to the one I'm fixing to tell you about.

If you're trying to watch your weight, stay out of restaurants. They're killers. You can be following a rigid diet, but when you go into the average restaurant, the closest thing you'll find is a cheeseburger and fries.

This is especially true at breakfast, since a low-calorie breakfast consists of coffee and maybe some juice. If that's all you have to start the day, by lunch you're hungry enough to eat the front seat of your car.

I was on a diet once when some friends told my wife about a new restaurant in Snellville. It was one of those Japanese restaurants where the guy actually cooks at your table. We were told that the food was excellent and not very fattening.

I had seen enough World War II movies to know that you very rarely see a fat Japanese, so I said, "What the heck. Let's do it. How can one little ole meal hurt my diet?" So we called Sukey's of Snellville and made a reservation for Saturday night.

When we arrived, the first thing they did was to take our shoes. I couldn't figure out why they did this, but they seemed real tickled to have our shoes. I guess they think that in some small, quiet, strange way they're evening up the score for Saipan.

Once they had our shoes, we were led to a table. The top of the table was actually a large grill with areas around the edges for eating. We were seated and offered a complimentary Japanese wine. It was hot and tasted like warm muscatel with just a dash of Draino.

Shortly afterwards, the chef made his appearance. He was wearing the traditional all-white Japanese chef's garb, which, when I thought about it, was exactly like the traditional all-white American chef's garb.

There were six people at the table, but he chose to take my order first. He turned to me and said, "What's for you, round eyes?"

I answered, "I resent that, Leon."

He smiled and said, "Excuse me, sir. I didn't mean to offend the imperialist dog, and besides, my name is not Reon."

He apparently decided that in the interest of time and international relations, he had better give everybody menus. The menu included a lot of things I'd never heard of, so I asked the chef a couple of questions.

"What's the John Wayne Steak?"

He smiled again and said, "It's big and tough."

"That doesn't sound too good," I said. "So what's the Exxon Shrimp?"

"They give you gas," he replied.

Then I spotted something that looked wonderful. I asked, "What do you get with the Yokohama Veal?"

"Excruciating stomach cramps," he answered with a smile.

He had pushed me far enough. I jumped up, screamed "Bonsai," and grabbed for his throat. He hit me upside the head with a large metal teapot. At least, I think it was a large metal teapot.

The next thing I remember was when I woke up in the parking lot without my shoes. All in all, I wouldn't recommend Sukey's of Snellville to my friends.

I've also had some interesting experiences at other ethnic restaurants. Following is a summary of some of those for your culinary illumination:

Italian

I love Italian food, but I try to stay out of Italian restaurants for two reasons: (1) Pasta and cheese are very fattening, and (2) I hate it when all the waiters keep trying to surrender to me.

Greek

All the food is delicious, but I have a lot of trouble with the menu. All the dishes sound like supporting actors in a foreign film.

Mexican

One of the main reasons I enjoy food from south of the border is that I have discovered the key to good service in Mexican restaurants. It's so simple I don't know why I didn't think of it years ago.

Newcomers to our country are very impressed when we try to speak their language. They don't seem to care whether you make sense or not, just as long as you make the effort. You'll be amazed at how much the service will improve if you do.

My favorite Mexican restaurant is located on Highway 78 between Loganville and Split Silk. It's called Casa Highway 78. Anytime I go there, I'm treated like a king; from Bambi Sanchez the waitress to Avery Ramirez the bus boy, they can't seem to do enough for me.

I recently explained my language/service theory to some friends, and they wanted to go the the Casa Highway 78 to test it. When we walked in, Bambi spotted me immediately and said, "Buenos tardes, Señor Porch."

I smiled back and said, "Thank you, Bambi, and Caesar Romero to you, too." She loved it. She laughed until she spilled a bowl of salsa.

Toward the end of a great meal, Bambi came up and asked, "Mas cafe?" Since she was holding a coffee pot at the time, I figured she was asking if we wanted more coffee. So I said, "Jas Juan Morcup." I don't know if Bambi got it, but she smiled anyway.

As we were leaving, my theory proven beyond a doubt, Bambi said, "Adios, Señor Porch."

And I answered, "Delores del Rio to you, too."

Yes sir, the folks at Casa Highway 78 love me. In fact, they love me so much that they've given me a pet Spanish name. When I go in now, they call me El Loco Gringo. I don't know what it means, but it sure has a nice ring to it.

Barbecue

Barbecue is not all that bad for a person trying to watch his weight ... if he sticks to the meat and avoids the bread. But I must warn you that as the popularity of barbecue has grown in recent years, some folks who don't know exactly what they're doing have gotten into the business.

Today a good barbecue joint is about as hard to find as a Kennedy button at a John Birch Society meeting.

Since I am acknowledged to be one of the country's few true experts on barbecue restaurants, I feel compelled to pass along to my readers a few rules about que-and-stew restaurants so you'll be able to tell the good ones from the imposters.

I should point out, however, that you may have trouble finding what I'm about to describe. Unfortunately, many of these places exist only in our memory.

Having said that, here are Ludlow's ten rules for a perfect barbecue joint:

1. There should be at least one waitress named Roxy and one named Hester. It is acceptable for these lovely ladies to work on separate shifts, but they must be on the payroll at the same time.

2. Waiters are unacceptable. All male employees, except for the busboy, must work behind the counter.

3. The only alcoholic beverage that can be sold on the premises is beer. Selling wine might attract the wrong kind of patron; anybody who would order wine with barbecue would kiss General Sherman on the mouth.

4. Barbecue must be the only thing on the menu. If they serve fried chicken or anything else, they cannot call themselves a true barbecue joint and should be picketed by the AFL/CIO and the Humane Society.

5. There should be religious slogans on the wall. The actual wording of the slogans is optional, but there should be at least one that says, "Repent or Burn in Hell!"

6. The bathrooms must be unfit for human use and should be out of order at least two days a week.

7. All soft drinks must be served in bottles. A

fountain soft drink is out of the question at a real barbecue joint. Mandatory brand names are Coca-Cola, R.C., Dr. Pepper, and Pepsi. In an effort to keep undesirables out, no diet soft drinks of any kind should be sold.

8. The cashier should keep a toothpick dangling from the corner of his mouth at all times. In certain areas of the rural South, a kitchen match may be substituted for the toothpick.

9. Every table must have a bottle of hot sauce on it. The only ingredients in the sauce should be vinegar, red pepper, and salt. The brand is optional, but it must have been produced in either New Iberia, Louisiana, or a place called Avery Island, Louisiana.

10. Beef is forbidden. It is perfectly acceptable in steak houses, Japanese restaurants, and rodeos, but beef has no place in a true barbecue joint. God gave the world pigs for one reason and one reason only: to be knocked in the head and barbecued until delicious. It is, indeed, the most noble of all beasts — a beast that asks little of man. It lives in squalor and eats anything that's served; it doesn't require a clean stall; it doesn't chase cars or cause you bad luck by crossing your path; it doesn't transmit rabies; and no unsuspecting cowboy has ever been trampled to death in a hog stampede. The pig lives but to serve. To offer beef in a barbecue restaurant would be an insult to all swinedom.

Heed these rules, and you'll never be disappointed

in your choice of a barbecue restaurant. Take it from someone who knows.

Soul Food

The term soul food means different things to different people, but to me it means good ole home-style cooking. It's my favorite kind of food in the world, and my passion for it accounts in large part for my large parts.

If I were scheduled to die in the electric chair tomorrow, I'd ask the warden to allow me to have soul food for my last three meals on earth. Here's what my menu would be:

Breakfast — Three scrambled eggs with cheese and Grits Grizzard, for openers. The grits dish is a delicacy invented by Lewis, Jr., and myself one morning about 4 A.M. after a long evening with our mutual friend, Mr. Jack Daniels.

Since I don't want to encourage anyone else to consume the calories which are part of Grits Grizzard, I won't give you the exact recipe; suffice it to say that it is made with sausage grease and is so good that it has been banned in most northern states and two foreign countries.

Along with my eggs and grits, I'd also have streak o' lean — a soul food staple. And, of course, no breakfast would be complete without cathead biscuits (so named because when they are properly prepared they're about the size of a grown cat's head).

This wonderful breakfast should be topped off by one-half cantaloupe, heavily peppered, and a large glass of sweet milk.

Dinner — This is actually the noon meal, but it should not be confused with lunch, which is only served north of Richmond, Virginia. My last dinner would consist of several meats, including country fried steak, pork chops, meat loaf, and Southern fried chicken. Vegetables (notice that I did not say veggies; anybody who says veggies is not worth the fatback it would take to cook a small pot of beans) would include a sampling of the following: Navy beans, pole beans, mashed potatoes, stewed tomatoes, butter beans, cucumbers soaked in vinegar, sliced tomatoes, spring onions, and fried green tomatoes.

Supper — I would repeat the dinner menu at this time, although I would add ham (prepared any way) and fried fish with hush puppies.

Dessert — Following dinner and supper, I would select from apple cobbler, peach cobbler, blackberry cobbler, rice pudding, apple pie, peach pie, egg custard, and (last but by no means least) the king of them all, banana pudding.

Gravy — Notice that I have created a special category for gravy. It is too special to be lumped in with anything else. Gravy can and should be eaten for breakfast, dinner, and supper. Also, any variety can be eaten — milky, sawmill, white, or red-eye.

Bread — Unlike gravy, only two varieties of bread

are acceptable with soul food — biscuits and corn-bread. The true test of a biscuit is, "Does it look, feel, and taste like Mama's?" If the answer is yes, then all you need is a dob of cow butter or some syrup. The same test can be applied to cornbread.

I don't want anyone to think that there are limitations on soul food menus. These are only my favorites — the dream meal of a man headed for the chair; you can choose your own. I grew up in a home where the cooking rule was mash it, fry it, and pour syrup on it. That's still the way it ought to be. Precious memories, how they linger.

All You Can Eat

In recent years, these restaurants have changed their advertisements from "All You Can Eat" to "All You Care to Eat." I don't know exactly what the difference is, but I presume the latter is some sort of attempt to remove the stigma of gluttony.

It doesn't work. We fat folks have been eating "all we can eat" all our lives, and calling it something different won't stop us now.

In truth, I'm not fond of these types of restaurants. They confirm what I have always suspected — that the average restaurant-going American is much more interested in quantity than quality. If you give him enough of it, he doesn't seem to care that the food has a certain concentration camp quality about it.

Allow me to prove my point. In many of these fat

factories, they require the customer to pay in advance, even before he has seen what they're serving. I find that mind-boggling. What if I don't like what they've decided to serve me?

I'm also offended by the signs prominently displayed on the walls. They warn against the dangers of stealing food or carrying it out of the restaurant. I always figured that anybody hungry enough to steal what barely passes for food needs it more than the restaurant.

Their wide selection of vegetables always tastes like they went straight from the can to the steam table. And the meats usually defy description or identification. The so-called sliced ham has more fat than a Weight Watchers' convention; the meatloaf contains more filler than a padded bra; and the chicken looked more appetizing in the barnyard.

I don't mean to condemn the innocent along with the guilty; I'm sure there are some smorgasbords where they care about the quality of the food. But a good rule of thumb is, If they want you to pay before you see the food, do an about-face.

Of course, if you're on a diet, you're better off staying out of restaurants anyway. They lead to the long-term pain of short-term gain.

'There is a vast difference
between a savage and a
civilized man, but it is
never apparent to their
wives until after breakfast.'

— *Helen Rolland*

8

When the Vigoro
Hit the Mixmaster

A WISE CHINESE philosopher once said, "To know where you are, you must first know how you got there."

I know that I'm overweight, and I know how I got there, but the knowledge doesn't seem to help very much. I guess that's why it's hard for Chinese philosophers to make a living.

I never had a weight problem in high school, even though I ate like the chief judge at a Pillsbury bake-off. Football and boxing were my passions, and those sports burned off all the calories I could consume.

Less than a year after high school graduation, I joined the Marine Corps, and they took over my eating as well as my exercise program. They did a good job, too; I weighed only about 170 when I was discharged.

But that's when the Vigoro hit the Mixmaster.

Ludlow Porch

My eating habits stayed the same as they had been for years, but my exercise suddenly was reduced to nil. The weight gain was slow at first, but after about five years I looked like the Mills Brothers had all moved into my body.

I looked up one day and found myself weighing 330 pounds. I had almost doubled my Marine Corps weight. I realized that if I didn't want to look like Kate Smith, I was going to have to start a serious diet.

Over the next several years, I tried one diet after another. Some were successful (I've lost more than two thousand pounds in my life), but others were not (I've gained most of it back).

But one thing was certain: When I became fat, my life changed forever.

Part II

BEING THERE

9

Shopping at Fulton Tent and Awning

ONE OF THE first indications that you've joined the ranks of the overweight is that your clothes no longer fit. That means when you finally manage to get the buttons through the holes, you have trouble breathing and your face begins to turn blue.

So then you go out and buy new, larger clothes (the old ones probably shrunk in the dryer), but no matter how much you spend, they just don't seem to look very good. For years I blamed my sartorial problems on clothing manufacturers; they just don't make attractive clothes for overweight people, I said.

Finally I had to break down and admit that it wasn't the clothes, funseekers. I was just too fat to look good in anything.

Like most fat folks, I made jokes about my weight to soften the blow. "I buy all my clothes from Fulton Tent and Awning," was one of my favorites. Or, "I'll just slip into a shower curtain and be right over." But in fact, shopping for clothes when you're into the super large sizes is about as much fun as falling down a flight of stairs.

The first problem you encounter is that most regular clothing stores don't carry a very good selection of large sizes. In men's clothing, you're lucky to find anything bigger than a size forty-eight on the rack, and most of them are about as stylish as zoot suits.

Faced with the option of becoming a nudist, you choose instead to go to a store for big men. The advantage of these stores is that they usually have a good selection of attractive clothes. The disadvantages, however, are enough to make a porpoise frown.

For openers, a shirt which cost fifteen dollars in a regular clothing store will cost you close to forty in a big men's store. There ain't *that* much more material in a size fifty-two than there is in an extra-large.

Then there's the clerks, who for some reason are always skinny. Having a skinny clerk in a fat man's store is like having a dentist work on your ingrown toenail. They just don't seem to grasp the problems of being overweight.

For example, they'll take your measurements and then announce in a voice loud enough for everyone in the store to hear, "Well, sir, it looks like you're going to need a size fifty-two portly." I, for one, would rather be called a fat bastard than to be called portly. I could settle for husky, obese, fat, or even lard bucket, but never, ever portly.

If you shop in a store for big men or women, there are certain universal rules which should be followed when buying clothes. I call these "Ludlow's Rules for Hiding It and Keeping It Hidden," and I'm glad to share them with you:

1. Never tuck your shirt or blouse into your trousers or skirt.

There are no exceptions to this rule. If you're fat, your best bet is to try and camouflage it. Tucking your shirt into your pants only emphasizes that you don't have a waist. Go instead for the loose look.

I used to know a young lady who, during her high school days, had a cute figure and dressed to show off the assets Mother Nature had bestowed upon her. When she got out of high school and entered the workforce, however, she cut back on her exercise but not on her eating.

The high school figure that she used to emphasize was gone almost overnight. Unfortunately, my friend didn't notice that the sand had shifted in her hourglass figure, so she continued to dress the same way she always had.

I can only assume that she thought the metric system was in some way responsible for the difference in the sizes of her clothes, and that humidity had warped all the mirrors on the face of the earth.

She continued wearing tight clothes with wide

belts, just as she had when she weighed fifty pounds less, and she tucked in all her blouses. The result was that she looked like she was wearing a money belt filled with Talmadge hams.

2. Never wear a bathing suit.

This shouldn't require any explanation. There's room enough in this world for only one great white whale, and Moby Dick is filling that spot.

3. Never wear horizontal stripes.

This is an old, tested rule for fat folks. Suffice it to say that wearing horizontal stripes makes us look like football fields.

4. Never wear tank tops.

At the very best, tank tops are tacky on a skinny person. On a heavy man or woman, they make the wearer look like a ten-pound sausage in a five-pound skin. They're a disaster.

5. Never wear short pants.

This rule applies to both men and women. A fat man in Bermuda shorts, invariably accompanied by black socks and wing-tip shoes, is one of the silliest sights in the world. I personally think such dress is responsible for the unfortunate decline of Miami Beach.

A fat lady in shorts is awful no matter what kind of

socks or shoes she wears. She looks bad enough coming towards you; going away, you get the illusion of two cats in her shorts fighting for their very lives.

6. Avoid wearing jeans.

Jeans are made for those who are slim of hip and lean of belly. So if you're built more like Orson Welles than James Stewart, forget about jeans, designer or otherwise. There ain't nothing you can write on the back pockets that will make you look any better in a pair of jeans.

7. Do not wear tennis dresses.

Fat men in tennis dresses are a little more than suspect. Fat women in tennis dresses are ridiculous; they look like they're wearing an umbrella tied at the waist.

8. Avoid large belt buckles.

With the urban cowboy craze came what I call the belt buckle craze. Men all over America started wearing large, silver belt buckles, which said things like "Lone Star State" or "Sam's Truck Stop."

Most of these buckles are about four inches by three inches, and some fat men think they make them look slimmer. The truth is that they make 'em look like they're wearing the grill of a '51 Hudson around their waists.

9. Don't wear high heels.

Fat men wearing high heels don't look any taller, but they do send out a message to the world: "I'm fat, but I hope that by wearing high heels you won't notice that I'm also short."

Fat women in high heels likewise don't look any slimmer; they just look a lot more uncomfortable. I always wonder how long they can maintain their balance.

10. Never wear bikini underwear.

Wearing bikini underwear can be very dangerous for people who are overweight. If you were in an accident and taken to an emergency room for treatment, you could die while the doctors and nurses stood around the room laughing at how silly you look in bikini underwear.

'Our grandmothers didn't have radio or television nor a car, but they had sense enough to keep covered up, and that's more sense than some modern women who carry their two hundred pounds and a pony tail to the grocery store in a pair of shorts.'

— *Dr. Pierce Harris*

'Corpulence makes a man reasonably pleasant and phlegmatic. Have you ever noticed that the nastiest of talents are invariably thin?'

— *Charles Laughton*

10

The Exorbitant
Price of Rudeness

ONE OF THE first things you learn upon entering
the fat world is that normally decent, God-fearing
folks can become rude, insensitive creeps in the presence of someone who is overweight.

To be fat is undesirable; to be rude is unnecessary,
unthinkable, and unacceptable.

When you're overweight, it's not unusual to hear
rude louts say such things as, "Just how much do you
weigh?", or, "Were your parents as fat as you are?"
But their favorite question seems to be, "Have you
ever thought of going on a diet?"

The answer is yes; anyone who is overweight
spends *most* of his time thinking about going on a
diet. We think about it every time we pass a full-
length mirror or every time we see a photo of our-
selves and realize what we really look like.

We think about it when buttons pop off our shirts

or seams start ripping out, and we think long and hard every time we walk up a long flight of stairs.

This sort of rudeness is particularly harmful when it's aimed at overweight kids. Adults can leave permanent scars with such comments as, "My, aren't you a roly-poly little girl," or, "You look just like the Pillsbury dough boy." From such insensitivity, kids start to feel socially unacceptable because they're fat.

I was once interviewing Cloris Leachman on my radio program. You probably remember Ms. Leachman as the woman who played Phyllis on the Mary Tyler Moore Show. She also won an Oscar for her brilliant performance as the coach's unfaithful wife in "The Last Picture Show."

Ms. Leachman is an aging actress with a bitchy streak as wide as Tyler, Texas. I had known her for less than five minutes when she stared at my ample girth with the appropriate amount of disgust and said, "Why did you let yourself get into this condition?"

Her mama apparently never told her that being rude is worse than being fat.

I learned two things from my interview with Ms. Leachman: (1) Her talent is overshadowed only by her rudeness, and (2) She is not bright enough to know that cruelty and rudeness never motivated anyone to lose weight.

If you know someone who is overweight and you care enough for them to worry about them, then care enough to know that they're more aware of their condition than you are. They may occasionally take a flip attitude about their weight, but deep inside they're miserable about it. The things you say, no matter how well intended, can only cause pain.

I knew a man one time who married his dream girl. It took him forty-five years to find her, but when he finally did, he was ecstatic. She was a tall, thin woman, quick to laugh and even quicker to smile.

She had a great personality, spoke several languages, and was at least his intellectual equal by any yardstick you wanted to use. It was easy to see that they not only loved each other but also were best friends.

One of the many things they had in common was that each loved to cook; in fact, cooking was their favorite hobby. Before long, as you might have guessed, she began to gain weight.

At first he made jokes about it and she just laughed. But slowly the remarks became more cruel than funny, and it became obvious to their friends that he was obsessed with her weight.

She felt his ire and was desperate to lose weight, but each time she tried to diet, he made fun of her attempts. After two years, they hated each other and subsequently divorced.

As it turned out, the fool really never had loved this wonderful woman; he had loved her body. He didn't enjoy her because she was good and decent and fun to be with; he enjoyed her in a pair of tight-fitting blue jeans. He didn't love her as a friend and a wife; he loved her as a possession, as a thing of beauty to show off to his friends.

Underneath her weight, she was the same charming woman — quick to laugh and quicker to smile. She was the same person who had simply gained weight.

It's a sad story, but it's one that has been repeated a thousand times. No amount of nagging or rude remarks will make a person lose weight, and just because a person is overweight doesn't mean they're any less loving or lovable.

If you can accept this fact, you're a special person. If you can't, you weren't much of a friend in the first place, and sooner or later your fat friend is going to tell you to buzz off and get the hell out of his or her life.

I hope this never happens to you. It's a mighty big price to pay for rudeness.

'All happiness depends on
a leisurely breakfast.'

— *John Gunther*

'Be careful about reading health books. You may die of a misprint.'

— *Mark Twain*

11

Ace Bandages vs. White Bell-Bottoms

PROBABLY THE MAJOR problem with being over-weight is that our health is jeopardized. We've been told all our lives that being fat can lead to high blood pressure, diabetes, and heart trouble, but it also makes any existing problem worse.

Just as we don't need anyone to tell us when we've gained weight, we also don't need anyone to tell us that we feel worse when we're overweight. Stairs seem steeper than ever; our jobs leave us exhausted after about three o'clock in the afternoon; we seem to spend more and more time sitting on the sofa.

The activities that we used to enjoy have been replaced by watching more television (our favorite show is usually "Cannon"). We would like to bowl, play tennis, or swim, but we just don't have the energy.

So threatened by various maladies, tired of sitting

on the sofa, and sick to death of television reruns, we finally decide to go to a doctor for help in losing weight.

Doctors who know what they're doing can be of great service to fat folks. They can give advice about how to take off pounds and remain healthy while you're doing it. But like all other professions, there are good ones and bad ones. They can range from Dr. Kildare to Dr. Jekyll.

The Dr. Jekyll — whom I prefer to call Dr. Clod — is easily recognized. He's the one who begins by telling an overweight patient that he's going to have a stroke and die because of his size. He says that obesity is the reason for all of the patient's medical problems.

Then when the fat patient is scared nearly out of his gourd and willing to try almost anything to lose some weight, Dr. Clod's only advice is, "Push away from the table a little sooner." Remember that I hate snotty doctors.

A doctor telling an overweight patient to push away from the table a little sooner is like telling a patient with a broken arm to go home and put a cast on it. If that's the best advice he has, then he can't help you lose weight any more than your gardener could.

Your next step should be out of his office like a young gazelle.

I had the misfortune several years ago to be involved with such a Dr. Clod. It all started on a Sunday.

Ace Bandages vs. White Bell-Bottoms

My family had decided that we would enjoy some ice cream after dinner, so I volunteered to go after it. As I was walking down the back steps, I tripped and fell. I threw my hands out in front of me to break my fall, but instead I almost broke both my wrists.

They started to throb and swell almost immediately. I was convinced that they were, indeed, broken. I called my family doctor, but he was in the hospital after having suffered a heart attack. I didn't want to bother any other doctor on a Sunday afternoon, so I decided to take a couple of aspirin and rough it until the next day.

I woke up the next morning with my wrists still swollen and also hurting, so I decided it was time to go to a doctor. I called several friends, hoping that one of them could recommend a good wrist doctor. On about the third call, I hit paydirt.

There was a new doctor in the area with a good reputation, so I called to make an appointment. The woman who answered the phone sounded like Broderick Crawford, but she said that if I'd come in about three o'clock, the doctor would see me.

By 2:30 my wrists hurt worse than a square kidney stone, so I showed up at the doctor's office ten minutes early. To my delight, the waiting room was empty, so I pressed the call button in hopes of fast service.

The woman who had sounded like Broderick Crawford also looked like him — about 6'1" and a solid 250 pounds. Her name tag said "Guts Benson."

She told me to sit down and said the doctor would see me shortly. I told her I was in a lot of pain and asked for some aspirin. "Aw, sit down and stop whining," she answered as she slammed the door shut.

I took my pained wrists to the nearest chair and sat down. Then I noticed for the first time that the office walls were covered from floor to ceiling with eight-by-ten color photographs of a man I presumed to be Dr. Clod. Although most of the pictures seemed to be taken in a war zone — the man was wearing fatigues and sporting a .45 automatic on his hip — Dr. Clod was smiling in each one. The man obviously likes his work, I thought.

Finally the door opened. I fully expected the nurse to say, "Set up a roadblock. Ten-four," but instead she directed me to a small room.

"Please get on the scales," she said. "We have to weigh you."

"Are you going to weigh all of me or just my hurt wrists?" I countered.

"Your crude Southern humor is out of place in a physician's office," she said. I was beginning to wonder if maybe I was out of place in this particular physician's office. When the scales finally settled down, she said, "Hummmm," and made a notation on a form attached to a clipboard.

Then she took my blood pressure and temperature. I explained that all I really wanted was for the doctor to look at my wrists — I could come back another day for a full going over. She smirked and left the room.

Forty-five minutes later — more than an hour after I had arrived — the doctor finally showed up. I was steamed, not to mention hurting.

As Dr. Clod came through the door staring at a clipboard, he was whistling "You'll Never Walk Alone." He was dressed in white bell-bottoms and a short sleeve, flowered Hawaiian shirt, and his hair hung down over his collar.

He also was just a touch over five feet tall.

Without ever looking up from his clipboard, he said, "Mr. Porch, you're fat."

I said, "Yes, Doctor, and you're short. Now, I can leave here and lose some weight, but what are you gonna do about your height?"

He tossed the clipboard aside and said, "I don't need your sarcasm."

"And I don't need your medical services," I answered. I was almost out the door when I decided to take one more shot. I looked back over my shoulder and said, "Give my best to Dopey and the other dwarves." He turned very white.

I learned another valuable lesson that day: Two shots of Jack Daniels and two ace bandages are better than a short doctor wearing white bell-bottoms and a flowered shirt.

'A vegetarian is a person who won't eat anything that can have children.'

— *David Brenner*

12

I'd Rather Eat Than Graze Any Day

ANOTHER SOURCE OF torment for fat folks is skinny folks. They're always around to remind us of what might have been.

The truth is, however, that people who are overweight and those who are underweight have a lot in common. For example, there are about as many skinny jokes as fat jokes:

— "He's so skinny he has to run around in the shower just to get wet."

— "She was so skinny that when she swallowed a pecan, six guys left town."

— "He's so skinny he can get into his T-shirt from either end."

— And when a woman is *real* skinny, people are prone to say, "The end doesn't justify the jeans."

Although I'm certainly no expert on being skinny, I do have a theory about the difference between us and them. Skinny people, it seems to me, have never discovered the wonders of late-night snacking on such culinary delights as potato chips, chocolate chip cookies, or an entire roast.

Instead, they have a strange, almost perverted desire for lettuce. Try as I might, I have never been able to understand their preoccupation with this almost tasteless first cousin to fescue. God only knows that I've tried to develop a taste for lettuce, but the only thing I've found in its favor is that it holds a lot of remoulade sauce.

I guess lettuce is the main reason I've never been fond of salads. No matter how many tomatoes or toppings you add, nothing seems to be able to overcome the taste of lettuce. That's why I don't understand the popularity in recent years of salad bars in restaurants.

I suspect salad bars are aimed primarily at those people who would rather graze than eat. And restaurant owners must love them, because they're able to sell thirty-five cents worth of lettuce for $4.50, plus they save on labor when the customer does all the work.

I was at a restaurant once and a waitress asked me if I would like to make my own salad. I said, "Only if you'll allow me to mix my own vodka tonic." She declined my generous offer.

Skinny people also seem to enjoy strange extracurricular activities, such as jogging. There are few things on earth skinny people like more than putting on tacky clothes and disrupting traffic alongside the road.

Some even carry radios with earphones when they run. This keeps them from being bored and also blocks out the noise of motorists, who are blowing their horns and screaming insults about the runner's mama.

There are many things about jogging that I don't understand. For example, why do some joggers wear their gym shorts outside their sweat pants? Now, that's tacky. And why do they never wash their shoes? Imagine what it must smell like inside their shoes after they've run five or six miles.

In an effort to broaden myself (intellectually only, you understand), I've asked many of my skinny friends who jog why they do it. The most common answer is, "Because it makes my heart beat faster." I've told them that a cigarette will do the same thing. Besides, I've spent the greater part of my life trying to find activities that would *not* make my heart beat faster.

My good friend Lardo Dupree went to his doctor recently for a check-up, and the doctor told him he was in absolutely horrible shape. The doctor said that he wanted Lardo to get back into the same condition he was in during his high school days, and that the only way he could do that was to start jogging ten miles a day.

Lardo promised to try and went out and bought himself some funny clothes and a pair of dirty, smelly shoes. Two weeks later he called his doctor and told him that he was 140 miles from home.

But I don't want to leave you with the impression that eating lettuce and jogging are the only strange things that skinny people do. Far from it.

I've got one skinny friend who likes to watch television in bed and snack. That in itself isn't too strange, but what he likes to snack on is radishes and salt.

He lies on his back, naked as a newborn bird, and fills his navel with salt. Then he dips the radishes into the salt.

Some skinny people can be disgusting.

'My idea of exercise is a good brisk sit.'

— *Phyllis Diller*

'No man is lonely while eating spaghetti.'

— *Robert Morley*

13

Thi Delta Tubbo — My Fraternity

SINCE THE BEGINNING of time, people with ideas and interests in common have sought each other out and joined together.

This clannish behavior probably started in the Garden of Eden. Adam and Eve became great friends, but not just because they were the only people there. You see, they shared a common interest. They both liked to get naked and eat apples.

The same is true of the people in the Mafia. They don't stick together just because of their Sicilian heritage. They also like to do the same things — they dress up in dark suits with wide-brimmed hats and kill people.

Winos stick together because they all enjoy getting drunk and urinating outdoors. Ball players get together off the field so they can have someone else to spit and scratch with. Scuba divers enjoy telling each other about how deep they do it, and religious groups get together to tell each other about how high they're going to go some day.

Fat folks are no exception. When the chips are down, one fat person will always stand arm-in-arm with his rotund brother or sister. I recently had this fact brought home to me in a delightful and surprising manner.

I had put my car in the shop for a little repair work, so my cousin Doodle offered to lend me his. I should point out here that my cousin Doodle is a race car driver, and his personal car is a new Corvette.

Doodle had this car tuned to the point that it would go about 150 miles per hour in his driveway.

I arrived at his house just after dark to borrow his car. I knew I couldn't stay long, 'cause I had to pick up my son at a Scout meeting. But in addition to being a generous fellow with his car, cousin Doodle is also a great host, and he wouldn't let me leave until we'd had at least one drink.

We had our one, but as I started to leave, Doodle's wife pulled a gun on me and insisted that I have two more. For the sake of domestic tranquility, I obliged.

Finally Doodle and his wife walked me out to the driveway, and Doodle began telling me how to drive his car. "First of all, don't put it in drive until you're ready to go, because it goes about sixty miles an hour while it's idling."

I turned the key, and when the engine kicked on,

you could feel the power right down to the seat of your pants. Like all people who like to drive fast, Doodle had backed his car into the driveway. I knew I was driving a bullet, so I barely touched the accelerator.

The tires squealed and the car jumped about six feet before it touched down. It startled me so that I stopped. Doodle walked up beside me and said, "Sweet, ain't she?"

I left Doodle's house feeling apprehensive about the fact that I was driving a car with more power than an Oral Roberts sermon and a dose of castor oil put together. But soon a very strange thing happened.

I was listening to the radio, and they were playing what the disc jockey called a "golden oldie dusty disc" — the immortal Hank Snow singing "I'm Moving On." I had not heard that wonderful song in years, and with the vodka splashing through my system, the words seemed more beautiful and meaningful than ever:

"See that big eight-wheeler rolling down the track, means your true loving daddy ain't coming back. I'm moving on. I'll soon be gone. You were flying too high for my little ole sky, so I'm moving on."

I thought to myself, Boy, they don't write 'em like that anymore. Magically, my mind shot back to my high school days. At that instant, as if by magic, the vodka and the Hank Snow music did that voodoo that they do so well. It happened in a heartbeat.

Ludlow Porch

Suddenly I was sixteen years old again. I had a crew cut and was wearing Levi's and penny loafers. The Corvette changed into a black 1940 Ford with a bumper sticker that said, "I may be slow, but I'm ahead of you." I felt great. I was young, driving fast, having a hell of a time.

I turned the radio up louder, flipped the air conditioning off, and rolled down the windows. Fresh air and Hank Snow music swept around me like a warm bath.

The entrance ramp to the expressway finally came up, and as I hung a sharp right, I said to myself, "Now let's see what this baby can do!"

I pushed the accelerator down. The faster I went, the better I felt.

"Mr. Engineer, with your throttle in hand, just take me on to the promised land. I'm moving on. I'll soon be gone. You're flying too high for my little ole sky. I'm moving on."

I had no idea how fast I was going, but it didn't matter anyway. The expressway stretched out in front of me, and on the radio Hank was coming to his big finish.

Suddenly I was jerked back to reality by the blue lights flashing behind me. In a flash the Ford, the Levi's, and the penny loafers were gone. The only things left were me, Doodle's Corvette, and the vodka. I felt a sinking feeling in my stomach.

I was resigned to my fate. I knew that within the

next thirty minutes I would be arrested, fin-
gerprinted, and thrown into some damp, under-
ground cell in the bowels of a nameless jail. I looked
warily into my rearview mirror, and just as suddenly
as they had come, all my fears vanished.

Getting out of the blue-lighted patrol car was my
boyhood friend and fellow tubbo, Fats Funderburk.

I hadn't seen Fats in years, but there was no mistak-
ing his huge frame. We had been so close in the old
days that I knew Fats would fix a murder rap for me if
I asked him to. I was so relieved that I decided to
play a little joke on my beloved Fats.

I just sat behind the wheel and left that huge motor
running. As Fats approached the car, his body filled
the entire rearview mirror. He was carrying a flashlight about two feet long, and I could tell that he was
irritated, because he was slapping it into his open left
hand.

Finally he was standing beside the door, feet spread
wide apart and still slapping the flashlight into his
palm. As I looked out the window, all I could see was
his belt buckle. It would have been a sign of subser-
vience for Fats to bend down and look into the car, so
he just stood there and I just sat there.

In a moment he spoke. "Let me see your drim liem,
boy." I don't know what it is about Southern cops,
but they always call driver's licenses "drim liem."

As I fumbled for my license, Fats said, "You got
any idea how fast you was going, boy?"

"No, I really don't," I said. "I was down in the engine room."

"Don't get smart with me, boy. I'll lock you up so long yo mama will forget yo name," he snapped back.

Playing my joke to the limit, I said, "That's the trouble with society today. Crime is rampant, but you cops are out here harrassing decent citizens."

"Decent citizens, my ass!" he screamed. "You was going damn near a hundred miles an hour!"

I figured the joke had gone far enough, so I handed my driver's license out the window. There was a moment of silence, then Fats bent over and looked through the window, smiling like an undertaker at a mass burial.

"Why, you ole sum bitch. I dang near busted you upside the head with my flashlight." I got out of the car, and we shook hands and hugged right there on the side of the expressway. "Let's me and you have us a little drink, Luddy," he said.

"Fine," I answered. "What time you get off work?"

Fats said, "I don't mean later; I mean now. I just busted a bootlegger, and I got some of the best two-day-old white lightning you ever sloshed over yo teeth. It'll put the white back in yo smile."

I thanked Fats for the offer but explained that I was already late picking up my son. We agreed to get together soon and test his haul. As I was driving away, Fats said, "You better be careful now, ya heah. You ain't far from the county line, and they got some police up there that's fanatical about how fast folks drive and how slow they talk."

Yessiree, when the chips are down and the going gets tough, one fat person can always depend on another one for help. That is, of course, unless there's only one pork chop left.

'A gourmet is just a glutton with brains.'

—*Phillip W. Haberman, Jr.*

Part III

GETTING
OUT OF
THERE

14

I'd Walk a Mile
For Potato Chips

A PERSON WHO is fat will do almost anything to lose weight — anything, that is, except eat less.

One of the first things we try is exercise. The theory is that if we burn off more calories, we can continue to eat and still lose weight. Unfortunately, many typical forms of exercise are not appropriate for those of us with a heavy persuasion. Allow me to give you a few examples.

Tennis

Tennis is not only wonderful exercise but also a lot of fun. It combines skill with sweating, and therefore burns off a lot of calories. That's why it is with deep regret that I report fat folks should not play tennis.

As the popularity of tennis has grown in recent years, style has become more important than the way you play the game. The influx of sissies into tennis also has affected the codes of proper dress on the courts.

Today, the need for a strong backhand has been replaced by the need for white shorts, a white knit shirt with some sort of animal's head on the pocket, and matching white socks and shoes. Unfortunately, such an outfit makes a fat person look like a large, grotesque noodle.

I've discussed women's tennis dresses before, so I won't bother to reiterate. Suffice it to say that even stretch nylon will stretch only so far before it rips.

Consequently, any health benefit which would be derived from playing tennis would be more than off-set by the public humiliation a fat person would feel from being dressed so silly.

Swimming

Swimming is a natural for us tubbos, and when done properly, it's great exercise for the entire body. In fact, fat people make such great swimmers that I don't know why more hefty men and women don't participate in the Olympics.

You see, it's very hard to sink a fat person. We float much better than skinny people. Seems to me that an overweight person would be a cinch to swim the English Channel; all we'd have to do is swim awhile and then float awhile. We could have someone alongside in a boat keep us supplied with sandwiches and potato salad to maintain our strength.

Sumo Wrestling

Sumo wrestling is a perfect exercise for fat men. The only equipment you need is a rubber band for your pony tail and a large leather jock strap.

On second thought, forget sumo wrestling.

Golf

Golf is probably the only sport with a piece of equipment that's designed especially for fat folks. It's called the golf cart.

Back in the old days, golf was great exercise and an effective way to lose weight. When a man walked eighteen holes and carried his own clubs, he burned a lot of calories. All that changed, however, one day back in 1923 on a golf course in Waco, Texas.

Two big ole boys had just finished eighteen holes and were absolutely exhausted. One of them was named Buford Cart and the other was named Rob Roy Westbrook.

They were lying on the floor of the clubhouse of the Festus Hagen Country Club, sweating like two Republicans in Massachusetts, when Rob Roy said, "Buford, I don't know about you, but I'm about worn out."

Buford said, "What you talking about! The last time I was this tired was when I rowed a boat from Dallas to Ft. Worth."

"But they ain't no water between Dallas and Ft.

Worth," said Rob Roy.

"No wonder I was so tired," said Buford.

They laid around on the floor for about forty-five minutes trying to get their breath back. Then Rob Roy said, "Buford, I got an idea! Tomorrow when we play, let's hire somebody to tote our golf bags. Then all we got to do is just walk."

Buford was so tickled with the idea that he went right out of the clubhouse and hired a teen-aged boy named Sidney Caddy to carry his clubs the next day. And until this very day in Waco, Texas, people who carry golf bags are known as Sidneys.

Rob Roy and Buford were pleased with their invention and enjoyed playing much more for awhile. But then one day Buford said, "You know, Rob Roy, the only thing I hate about golf is all that walking. If we could think of a way to eliminate that, golf would be a hell of a game."

"By George, I think I've got it," said Rob Roy. "Tomorrow when we play, we'll ride horses and let Sidney follow along behind us. The only time we'll have to get down is to hit the ball."

The next day after their round of golf, they were sitting in the clubhouse having a sandwich — they called it a club sandwich, of course — when the membership committee came in. Seems that Rob Roy and Buford had torn the course up something fearful with their horses, so the membership committee took both of them outside and lynched 'em.

As with all great men, however, it was easier to kill them than to kill their ideas. As a result of the publicity which followed their being lynched, scientists around Texas got busy and invented the golf cart — named partially, of course, for the late Buford Cart.

Since the invention of the golf cart, the game has been a lot more fun but a lot less exercise.

Obese Dog Sled Racing

Dog sled racing is a great way to lose weight. There are, however, some variations on standard dog sled racing that must be used by the obese dog sled racer. Allow me to explain.

After the first race, dogs tend to become very resentful about pulling a fat person around in the snow. They usually manifest this anger by turning on their fat driver and tearing him into bite-size chunks.

This unfortunate occurrence almost certainly will hold down interest in obese dog sled racing. Therefore, any fat person who wants to participate in this sport should do so without dogs. I can guarantee that by pushing a dog sled, you will exercise every muscle in your body.

If you're lucky enough to live in an area without snow, so much the better. You can get even more exercise with the same number of hernias.

Boxing

One certainly can get a lot of exercise by boxing.

The only drawback is that the skinny fellow with quick hands in the ring with you probably will get even more exercise by beating your brains out.

Skiing

You really don't get much exercise skiing downhill. On the other hand, falling down and trying to get back up in all that snow is a lot of exercise.

If you're adept enough that you don't fall when you ski, then there's one more thing you need to be aware of: inertia.

My friend Enrico Wilkie, who weighs 320 pounds, went skiing recently in Aspen, Colorado. When Enrico started down the slope, he suddenly realized that his ample poundage made him go faster than the other skiers. Unfortunately, he had failed to take this into consideration.

By the time he reached the bottom of the slope, Enrico was traveling about seventy miles an hour and was completely out of control. He already had lost both his ski poles and a cap which said "Tuberose Snuff."

He wiped out a brick barbecue pit and did $1,800 damage to a condo once owned by John Denver. When last seen, Enrico was on the outskirts of town still picking up speed.

Free-lance Exercise

Since many forms of traditional exercise are not

suitable for fatsos, we sometimes have to create our own.

My high school friend Wanda Sue Fonda always got her exercise by going to the Chateau Switchblade. Three times a week she would put on her leotards, drop four quarters in the jukebox, and for the next three hours she would dance on the tables and eat raw wienies. She said the music made her dance and that nothing on earth gave her more energy than raw wienies.

I guess my favorite free-lance exercise is one called the Bumper Rip. I must warn you, however, that this exercise is not for the fainthearted.

The Bumper Rip was invented by accident in 1962 at the annual Poke Salet Festival in Snellville, Georgia. Johnny Walker Stevens had been celebrating at the festival, and by about three o'clock in the afternoon he was bad drunk.

Johnny Walker, a big ole boy, was bad to show off when he got drunk, so he decided it would be great fun to rip the bumper off the mayor's car. Well, he had so much fun that he had somebody put a stopwatch on him while he ripped two doors off Mrs. Wiggins's '56 DeSoto.

One thing led to another, and by dark there wasn't a car in Snellville with both bumpers in place. From that humble beginning came the Bumper Rip.

I would like to offer a little advice before you try the Bumper Rip yourself, however: (1) You should be at least two-thirds drunk before you try it, and (2) Always start small and work your way up. For example, you could begin by tearing off a windshield wiper or two, then move up to radio antennas, then side-view mirrors, and then a front bumper off a small Japanese import. If you still have the urge after that, you can tackle a full-size bumper.

'The only reason I would take up jogging is so that I could hear heavy breathing again.'

— *Erma Bombeck*

'I don't jog. If I die, I
want to be sick.'

— *Abe Lemmons*

15

What You Lose
At a Spa Is Green

AFTER A PERSON has failed to lose weight through unsupervised exercise, such as those discussed in the previous chapter, the next move is usually to join a spa.

You've seen all the ads on television and in the newspapers, where everyone at the spa is young, tanned, and built like either Arnold Schwarzenegger or Bo Derek, and you know that's what you want to look like.

I've seen all those ads, too. Judging from them, I assumed you couldn't join a spa unless you were under twenty-five, tanned, and very pretty. I've never seen anybody who looked like me in a single one of those ads.

But the truth of the matter is that they'll sell that dream to anybody who'll buy it. And that's just what most of us fatsos are looking for — a dream that will let us eat a whole coconut cake and still be slim.

The only person I ever knew who had a quick weight loss at a health spa was my friend Spiro Lewis. He lost ten pounds on his first visit. You see, Spiro busted a gut trying to show off for a tanned young girl, and in emergency surgery they removed his appendix and twelve feet of small intestine. Net loss: ten pounds.

For most of us, however, the only thing we lose at a spa is money. After being hooked by the aforementioned ads, you visit a spa at a cheap introductory price. First they invite you into a small room where you will sweat.

I'm not talking about a steam room. I'm talking about a small sales office where you're hot-boxed. A guy who's built like a Roman statue starts by explaining that you can no longer function as a decent human being or be a respected member of your community if you don't belong to his particular spa.

Then he opens a door to reveal a long, black hearse backed up to it. He says that if you're foolhardy enough not to join, every malady known to medical science will descend upon you, and you probably won't live long enough to make it to the door. Should that happen, he says he'll be glad to carry you that far.

You should know, however, that very few people who join a spa ever go enough to achieve any results. If all the people who belong to any given spa showed up at the same time, it would look like the Third

World had just arrived at the doorstep.

I was a member of a spa for awhile. I became a member by giving them a lot of money for a lifetime membership. They're now bankrupt and out of business, so I can only presume that a lifetime membership meant theirs, not mine.

Actually, I didn't really mind when they folded since I hadn't lost any weight when I went. But I did sort of miss the people-watching, because a spa is one of the best places in the world to watch folks.

People who go to health spas generally fall into one of two categories. The first group, and the largest, is the young fellows who spend fifty percent of their time pumping iron and the other fifty percent looking into the mirrors which adorn every flat surface.

I always felt that anyone whose neck and waist were the same size was sort of silly looking, but apparently that's what these fellows are after. They all wear T-shirts about a size too small, and they spend a lot of time talking about their "pecs." I think that's their chests.

I know times have changed a lot of things, but when I was growing up, a fellow was more interested in the size of his girlfriend's chest than in his own. Precious memories, how they linger.

The second category of folks at the spa is made up of the people I call middle-age crazies. These are the guys who woke up one morning, realized they were forty years old, and for some strange reason thought life had passed them by.

They immediately bought a sports car, some cowboy boots, and joined a spa in hopes of looking the same in their Levi's as they did twenty years earlier. They're easy to spot — they're the ones with the new toupee or the recent hair transplant.

Their favorite thing to wear in the steam room is a rubber rain suit. They're trying to sweat off not only pounds but also years. It never works.

There's one thing about these guys that always amazes me: They'll work out and sit in the steam room for a couple of hours, and then they'll leave together to go get a beer and some pizza. Sounds like my kind of diet, but then their results are a lot like mine, too.

People-watching in the steam room is a lot more haphazard. When everyone is sitting there with nothing more than a towel covering them, it's hard to tell who's who ... or what.

Once when I was sitting in the steam room, I suspected that one of the fellows in there with me was gay. The tip-off was that he sat there spraddle-legged singing "Some Enchanted Evening."

Another time I had a terribly embarrassing experience in the steam room. I was there with my friend Gene, whose mouth is about as dirty as a free-running sewer. His language is so filthy it could embarrass a pimp convention.

Gene started to tell this awful joke — a long, awful joke. It went on and on. The fellow sitting across from us listened politely but didn't laugh when Gene finally delivered the punch line. We figured he was just worn out.

Later when we were dressing in the locker room, we saw why he didn't laugh. He was a Catholic priest. Gene said there ought to be a law requiring priests to wear at least their collars in steam rooms. I agreed.

If you're still thinking about joining a spa, I'd like to point out two other things: (1) You probably didn't gain weight because of a lack of exercise; you probably gained weight because you were eating with both hands, and (2) The best part of joining a spa is that they don't require you to attend.

'The best way to lose
weight is to get the flu and
take a trip to Egypt.'

— *Roz Lawrence*

16

The Marquis de Sade Diet Plan

HAVING TRIED AND failed with supervised and unsupervised exercise, the next move for a person anxious to lose weight is gimmicks.

I don't know anyone who has been overweight for a long time who hasn't tried at least one gimmick. Some of them sound outrageous, but you must remember that those of us on the top side of the Toledo can get pretty desperate.

I saw a television commercial recently that portrayed a lady trying to squeeze into a dress that was obviously too small for her. In fact, she couldn't have gotten into this dress with Vaseline and a shoe horn.

The announcer said, "Has this ever happened to you? Only one hour before the party and you can't fit into your favorite party dress." He then goes on to explain that now you can buy something called "slim-wrap" and lose up to six inches in your hips, legs, and arms in about one hour.

While he's talking, on the bottom of the screen in little bitty letters it says, "This loss of inches is temporary." Then it says in real big letters that Mrs. K.R. of Perth Amboy, New Jersey, lost eight inches while she slept, and that Mrs. Z.L. of Valley Rock, North Dakota, lost seven inches while she was watching a "Gentle Ben" rerun.

Finally they hit you with another one of those famous guarantees. They say in huge letters that if you don't lose at least six inches off your waist, legs, and arms, they'll send you another supply of "Slimwrap" absolutely free.

Think about it: If it doesn't work, they'll send you some more so it can not work again. Some guarantee.

What I kept thinking about was, Just how temporary is this loss of inches? I have this vision of the fat lady losing enough inches to get into her favorite party dress, then going to the party and having all the inches, lumps, and bumps come back suddenly. That could be embarrassing.

Suppose the dress disintegrated all at once. Or suppose the seams held up and the poor fat lady got squeezed to death because her dress was too tight.

Another thing that bothered me was, What do they wrap you in? It seems to me that a secondhand B.F. Goodrich inner tube would work as well as anything.

I also wanted to know, Does it chap you? It's pretty painful and unpleasant to have chapped lips, but I bet a chapped body would hurt worse than stumping your toe on a stob.

When President Nixon re-opened relations with China several years ago, acupuncture became the rage. Almost every newscast had a story about some Chinese doctor sticking needles into a patient to stop pain, relieve tension, or cure shingles.

It didn't take fat folks long to figure out that they might be able to lose weight the same way, and they started flocking to acupuncturists.

Here's how it was supposed to work:

First you went to a Chinese guy, usually a man named something like Wha Wen Wong. Although Mr. Wong advertised himself as an acupuncturist, he could have been an out-of-work plumber or a defrocked monk for all you knew.

Mr. Wong then would put a device in your ear, and anytime you got hungry, all you had to do to kill your appetite was pull on it. For this you paid forty bucks.

What Mr. Wong and the others didn't understand, however, was that people who are overweight don't eat just because they're hungry; they frequently eat because they love the taste of food. Tugging on a device sticking in your ear might kill your appetite, but it won't kill the desire for a Hershey bar.

My favorite new gimmick is hair analysis. This operates on the premise that people overeat because their bodies are trying to replenish some vitamin or mineral that's missing from their diet. A chemical analysis of the hair is supposed to tell you which vitamins and minerals to take so that you won't be hungry anymore.

For an extra forty dollars, they probably can tell you the color of your hair, too.

I haven't tried this system, but I'd bet the farm that these people just happen to sell the vitamins and minerals that their tests say you need. I suspect most of the weight you're going to lose at one of these places will be out of your wallet.

Either way, it's going to be an expensive haircut. I can't help wondering if this is how the term "clip joint" made its way into the language.

Hypnosis is another gimmick sometimes used to try to lose weight. I tried it once, mostly out of curiosity, but I thought it was a little silly.

The hypnotist explained to me in advance that I would not be aware when I was "under." He was right about that. I may still be under for all I know, because I was wide awake during the whole session.

He kept talking to me real soft and low, very much like Ronald Coleman used to talk to Irene Dunne. He told me I was resting on a puffy white cloud that was drifting slowly in a blue summer sky.

He said that when he snapped his fingers, I would feel better than I had ever felt before and, most importantly, I would have no desire to overeat. He told me several other things, all designed to plant the suggestion in my mind that food isn't all that great, and that overeating is bad for me.

Then he told me again how good I would feel when I woke up. I thought that was pretty strange, since I was wide awake at the time.

Whatever he was trying to do didn't work, because I didn't lose my desire to eat or lose any weight. As with so many of these gimmicks, the only thing I lost was a little cash.

I hesitate to call this next subject a gimmick, since it seems to have worked for many people. But what the heck — it's my book. I'm referring, of course, to programs you join where they provide all of your food, except water. You don't put anything in your mouth that you don't buy from them.

I was on this diet for thirty days and lost thirty pounds. Sounds great, right? Wrong! It was the most horrible thirty days of my life. While some people could tolerate the diet food, I found it compared unfavorably to liver-flavored cardboard.

There also was a diet drink that you made with water and fruit-flavored powder. I would compare its taste to that of drinking Iranian sweat several times a day.

When I went on this diet, I was determined to lose weight, so I forced down the entrees as long as I could. When that became unbearable, I just didn't eat. That's not a healthy way to diet.

I'm glad this technique works for some folks, but I found it to be an expensive way of torturing myself.

A far more pleasant gimmick for losing weight seems to be very popular with movies stars, socialites, and assorted chubby rich people. It's called the health farm or the dude ranch, although I prefer to call it the fat farm.

Here's how a fat farm works: First you send them a lot of money. Then you go there and you're put up in a fancy room and waited on hand and foot. They have daily exercise classes and all sorts of outdoor activities — swimming, horseback riding, volleyball, and anything else that will burn calories and not seem like torture.

The only food you get is low-calorie; they control what you get and how much you get. There are no candy or drink machines at the end of the breezeways. If you stay there long enough (or if your money holds out long enough), you definitely will lose weight.

Unfortunately, that's too big a price to pay for most of us tubbos.

Finally, there are two other methods of losing weight which I've seen people try. These definitely are not gimmicks; they're acts of desperation, and I don't recommend either of them.

The first is having your mouth wired shut. I knew a lovely lady once who tried this. Her dentist put braces on her teeth and wired her mouth shut so that only a straw would fit between her lips. Liquids were the only thing she could eat.

It worked. After several weeks she lost the weight she intended to lose. We were all very proud of her for the courage she displayed.

About a year later, I invited her and her husband to a party we were having at the radio station. She declined at first, but when I insisted, she finally admitted that she just didn't want to see me — she had gained back all the weight she had lost.

I almost cried, not because she had gained back the weight (I had done that many times), but because this lovely lady thought I would judge her by her weight.

Having her mouth wired shut had taken off pounds, but it had not altered her eating habits or her mental attitude about food.

The second act of desperation is the bypass operation. Every doctor I asked about this surgery said it should be performed only in life-threatening situations or cases of morbid obesity. (Morbid obesity, by the way, means at least one hundred pounds over your ideal body weight. Ideal body weight can be figured by allowing one hundred pounds for the first five feet of height and then adding five pounds for each inch.)

Morbid obesity in itself is certainly life-threatening, since the mortality rate for such people is eleven times higher than normal. But in the case of the bypass operation, the cure can be worse than the disease.

The procedure results in the body's expelling food quickly and in a poorly digested form. Seventy-five to ninety percent of the patients who have this operation lose sufficient weight; another one to six percent die.

The surgery also can lead to liver disease, lengthy diarrhea, arthritis, gallstones, and so forth. It's not a pleasant option.

If you think you're this desperate, talk long and hard with your doctor. My advice is first try another diet or even another gimmick.

'The first time I see a jogger smile, I'll try it.'

— *Joan Rivers*

'Your body is the baggage you must carry through life. The more excess baggage, the shorter the trip.'

— *Arnold H. Glasgow*

17

Has Anybody
Seen My Elephant?

A Dieter's Prayer

This is my prayer as I contemplate my belly: Dear Lord, please save me from doughnuts with jelly. And Lord, please keep me from that fattening brew — Budweiser, Pabst, and Miller Lite, too.

Please, Lord, stop my craving for my wife's home-made bread, and help me to realize that it's all in my head. Take away my yearning for a big juicy steak and, above all, the things that the baker bakes.

Hear my prayer, O Lord, each word as it's given, so someday I'll look just like David Niven.

O Lord, hear this prayer, each word that I utter, and if you're really listening, Lord, please pass the butter.

WHEN ALL ELSE has failed — the exercise and all the gimmicks — there's only one thing left for a fat person to try. A diet.

As I said earlier, I have been on many diets in my lifetime. In fact, I have lost more than fifty pounds more times than I remember, and all told I have lost more than two thousand pounds. But if you'll take a quick look at the picture on the cover of this book, you'll see that my battle is not over yet.

Nonetheless, dear reader, I want to share with you some of the more successful diets that I have tried.

Dr. Brezil's Famous Fish Diet

This diet is based on eating a lot of protein. You eat broiled fish three meals a day. I lost weight trying it, but after a week I had an uncontrollable craving for worms. I don't recommend this diet unless you own stock in a bait shop.

Diet Pills

I've had some good results with pills. For awhile they seem to kill my appetite and cut down on my craving for fattening foods. I also noticed that they give me a lot of energy. Once, for no good reason, I found myself painting my garage at four o'clock in the morning. Another time I caught myself driving seventy-five miles an hour down Peachtree Street, and I wasn't in any particular hurry.

Dr. Feldman's Diet

On this diet, you can have anything you want to eat. The only stipulation is that you must hold your breath the entire time you're eating. I lost a good deal of weight on Dr. Feldman's diet, but I never got used to fainting.

The Porch Elephant Diet

I invented this one myself, and it's a sure-fire way to lose weight. You can eat one elephant a week, cooked any way you like, but you must catch it yourself and kill it with a butter knife. I found that after the first week I just laid around on the living room floor with a butter knife in my hand, screaming for elephants. For variety after the first week, you may substitute a cocker spaniel for the elephant.

Weight Watchers

This is truly a fabulous diet. The first time I tried it, I was faithful and lost about sixty pounds in a relatively short period of time. The good thing about Weight Watchers is that you get enough to eat while you're dieting.

In addition to the diet, they try to teach behavior modification; that means they try to teach you to stop eating like you're going to the electric chair.

I must admit I was less successful with my behavior modification. My first day off the diet, I ate the First Methodist Church in Snellville and two tickets to a

Conway Twitty concert.

The Ex-Lax Diet

This is another diet I invented. The advantage of it is that you can eat anything you want — bread, butter, potatoes, cakes, pies, or whatever. The only drawback is that along with your meal you must eat a full box of Ex-Lax.

The secret to this diet is that although you can eat anything you want, after three days you're too weak to walk to the table. This diet comes with two guarantees: (1) You will lose weight, and (2) You will end up in the hospital. Check your hospitalization plan before trying this diet.

The Drinking Man's Diet

This diet calls for drinking a fifth of Jack Daniels thirty minutes before each meal. You may not lose much weight, but you'll experience many happy hours.

The truth is that alcohol *is* very caloric. For example, a beer with four percent alcohol has roughly two hundred calories per twelve ounces. Three cans of that will knock a hole clean through a 1,500-calorie-per-day diet.

The same is true of wine. At eighteen percent alcohol, you're looking at about 165 calories per one-half cup. If you're one of those who drinks straight from the bottle, you're in trouble.

Gin, rum, vodka, and whiskey which are about eighty-six proof contain about seventy calories per shot. That may not sound like much, but don't forget the calories in the mixers.

My boyhood friend Snake Burnett was very weight conscious, but Snake couldn't do without a little snort everyday. So he searched far and wide for a diet that would allow him to drink. He asked his doctor about it, and the doctor suggested that he get lots of exericse. That posed another problem for old Snake, 'cause he hated exercise more than Nixon hated tape recorders.

The only regular exercise Snake ever got was fist-fighting on Friday nights at Monk Gregory's Billiard Palace. So Snake wrote a letter to the trainer of the Ohio State wrestling team and asked him to estimate how many calories were burned up in an average fist-fight.

With that information in hand, Snake quickly calculated that if he got into two fist-fights and one riot, he could drink one fifth of whiskey and one six-pack of beer per weekend without gaining weight.

Snake forgot to calculate how many more calories would be burned up as the police beat him senseless, but by then it really didn't matter anyway. One thing he did learn, however, is that a blackjack upside the head usually will kill an appetite.

The Yogurt Diet

This is one of the most disgusting diets I have ever run across. The name alone should tip you off. Just say it out loud — YOGURT. It sounds more like a bodily function than a food.

Besides that, if fat people liked yogurt they probably wouldn't be fat in the first place.

This diet was developed by Willetta Warburg, a food editor, and Rose Mirenda, a nutritionist. It gives you a seven-day menu that is high in lean protein and low in cholesterol, saturated fats, and refined carbohydrates (that's Twinkies, for those of you who don't like science).

For example, here's one day's menu that contains about a thousand calories:

Breakfast — One small glass of prune juice; one container of plain yogurt; one slice of whole wheat toast; one small pat of margarine; one plain cup of coffee or tea.

Mid-morning Snack — Four dried apricot halves.

Dinner — Four canned sardines, drained of oil; one-half hard-cooked egg; a wedge of lettuce; a slice of tomato; one slice of whole wheat toast; one cup of plain coffee or tea.

Mid-afternoon Snack — A container of plain yogurt.

Supper — Three slices of breast of chicken, baked or broiled or stewed, plus the liver; one-half cup of cooked spinach; one-fourth cup of rice; one cup of plain coffee or tea.

Bedtime Snack — One glass of skim milk.

That, funseekers, is probably the most tasteless diet ever devised. After a full week of eating this, you would not only hate plain yogurt, but you'd also probably hate America, the works of George Gershwin, and your mama.

The Blue Diet

On this diet, you can eat all the blue food you want. The catch is that there isn't any blue food.

Man, of course, has created enough dyes to make anything blue, but Mother Nature, in her infinite wisdom, did not see fit to make any food naturally blue. No, not even blueberries; they're actually purple, and there's no blue in the meat of the blue fish.

So go ahead — eat all the blue food you want.

'A fat paunch never breeds fine thoughts.'

— *St. Jerome*

18

The Power of Disgusting Thoughts

IF YOU HAVE spent much time dieting, you undoubtedly have faced what I call the moment of truth. This usually comes late in the evening, when you think you can't go another minute without something to eat.

In my opinion, this is make-it-or-break-it time for dieters. If you can find something to take your mind off food, there's a chance you can make it to bed without blowing your diet.

Over the years, I have found several diversions which might work for you. Try one of these the next time you get the munchies at night:

1. Perform an autopsy.
2. Dip your mangy dog in used motor oil.
3. Stand naked in front of a full-length mirror and do side-straddle-hops.
4. Go to the store and try on bathing suits.

5. Go to the police station and confess to a murder. Any murder.

6. Call you ex-wife on the phone.

7. Get a couple of estimates on being circumcised.

8. Change your transmission fluid.

9. Eat some ice.

10. Give your cat an enema.

11. Gargle with aftershave lotion.

12. Turn your mother in to the IRS.

13. Clean the bird cage.

14. Bathe your goat.

15. Gut a squirrel.

16. Tease an alligator.

17. Drink a vodka and mayonnaise on the rocks.

If you're still hungry after trying one of these diversions, you should be working with the sanitation department. If after trying two of these you've still got your appetite, I'll call and reserve a space for you in the zoo.

'Cheese — milk's leap
toward immortality.'

— *Clifton Fadaman*

'If God had meant for us to travel tourist class, he would have made us narrower.'

— *Martha Zimmerman*

19

Have Faith — It Just Might Work

DURING THE LAST half decade, there must have been a million diet books printed, and at least three or four million weight loss products have been offered to the overweight public.

But when it's all read and said, the only successful diets are those that work. Each person has to figure out, usually through trial and error, which program or gimmick works best for him or her.

My good friend Hal Hayes is a perfect example of this. Hal, who is known throughout the South as a sportswriter and public relations man supreme, grew up during the second World War and was raised by loving grandparents.

Like most of those who lived through the Great Depression, Hal's grandparents thought it was almost sinful to waste food.

When Hal's plate was piled high with the wonderful

things that only a Southern grandmother can prepare, she would always tell him, "Son, you know there's a war going on, and if you don't eat everything on your plate, Hitler will come and take your leftovers and feed them to his evil Nazi troops. Then they'll grow strong and kill our brave American soldiers."

In Hal's young mind, a strong seed was planted. Even at such a tender age, Hal was a patriot and wanted to do his part to win the war. His plan was simple: He was too young to fight, but he would clean his plate at every meal and try to starve the bastards to death.

He not only ate everything on his plate, but he also ate anything left on anybody else's plate. Towards the end of the war, when young Hal finally realized that Hitler was not going to come to Boaz, Alabama, it was too late.

Hal had developed eating habits that one day would send his weight soaring to more than five hundred pounds. If you're looking for a silver lining to this cloud, remember that we won the war.

When Hal weighed more than five hundred pounds, he encountered all sorts of problems. For example, Hal was a sportswriter who had to travel a lot, and I can assure you that a five-hundred-pound man will not fit into a single airplane seat. And there's never been a restaurant chair which would hold a five-hundred-pound man.

Hal had a great sense of humor and joined everyone else in jokes about his size. But inside this wonderful man was going through pure hell. He tried every diet anyone suggested, but ultimately his bad eating habits overcame his good intentions.

Fortunately for Hal, he had inherited more than bad eating habits from his grandmother; he also had inherited her deep love for God and the faith that prayer would sustain you when nothing else seemed to work.

One Wednesday night at prayer meeting, Hal had an experience that would change his life forever. The sermon that night was about prayer and faith moving mountains. In the middle of the sermon, the preacher made eye contact with Hal and said in a soft, reassuring voice, "Prayer and faith can move that mountain from your chest."

It seemed to Hal to be a personal message from God, a message saying that God loved him and knew what he had been going through. When Hal prayed that night, he said, "Lord, fill me with your love, give me whatever I need to lose this weight. Please, God, help me. I'm in your hands."

The weight started coming off — first five pounds, then ten. For the first time in his life, Hal began losing weight. He had a compulsion to walk two or three miles a night. Hal proceeded to lose 268 pounds.

The first time I saw him after his incredible weight

Ludlow Porch

loss, I asked, "Hal, how did you do it?"
He smiled and said, "Faith, Ludlow, just faith."
If it worked for Hal Hayes, it might work for you.

'I consider exercise vulgar.
It makes people smell.'

— *Alec Yuill Thornton*

'Never trust a skinny cook.'

— *Ludlow Porch*

20

Tubby Trivia

HERE'S A SELECTION of trivia questions relating to food and those who love it. Test your knowledge:

1. What comic strip character was a hamburger lover?

2. In the comic strip "Bringing Up Father," what was Jiggs' favorite food?

3. What was Jiggs' favorite restaurant?

4. On the Roy Rogers television show, what was the name of Dale's restaurant?

5. In the Bowery Boys movie series, what was the full name of the man who owned Louie's Sweet Shop?

6. What was Peter Gunn's favorite bar and restaurant?

7. What was Matt, Festus, Kitty, and Doc's favorite restaurant on "Gunsmoke"?

8. Name Popeye's favorite food.

9. On radio, where did "the elite meet to eat"?

10. Who was Windy Halliday?

11. Who was the cook on the Ponderosa?

12. In the comic strip "Smiling Jack," one of the characters was so overweight that his shirt buttons constantly popped off. What was his name?

13. Who was the heaviest president of the United States?

14. What is the principle ingredient of Welsh Rarebit?

15. What comic strip featured a character named Tubby?

16. Who sang the hit record, "Too Fat Polka"?

17. What is the only food that has its seeds on the outside?

18. The smallest seed is the mustard seed. What is the largest seed?

19. What is the most difficult food for your body to digest?

20. Where do we get cashew nuts?

21. What is the most popular condiment in America?

22. What are the first names of Baskin and Robbins?

23. In order, what are the three most popular flavors of ice cream in America?

24. What comic strip character is credited with creating the multi-level sandwich named for him?

25. Where does saffron come from?

26. Who was Gil Favors's cook?

27. Where do grits come from?

28. Who puts sugar on grits?

29. What do you get when the recipe calls for equal parts of flour, salt, and water?

30. Who wrote the first cookbook with standard measurements?

31. What company uses the most sugar in the world?

32. How long is the shelf life of unpopped popcorn?

33. Who's favorite food was a Bronto Burger?

34. On "Laverne and Shirley," what was Shirley Feeney's favorite drink?

35. Where did Archie Andrews hang out?

36. Who was The Great Gildersleeves's cook?

37. Who was the cook at Camp Swampy?

38. Who was Gomer Pyle's mess sargeant?

39. Name the cook on television's M*A*S*H.

40. What is Garfield's favorite food?

41. Who owned the Jot-Em-Down Store?

42. Who was Gene Autry's chubby sidekick?

43. On television, who was Wild Bill Hickok's chubby sidekick?

44. Who was Joe Palooka's overweight friend?

45. What former heavyweight contender was so fat that his nickname was "Two Ton"?

46. What famous golfer was at one time referred to as "Ohio Fats"?

47. What movie star was known as "The Fat Man"?

48. In the comic strip "Buzz Sawyer," who was

Ludlow Porch

Buzz's overweight sidekick?

49. On television's "Alice," who is the owner of Mel's Diner?

50. In "Casablanca," what was the full name of Rick's cafe?

Tubby Trivia Answers
1. Popeye's friend Whimpy
2. Corned beef and cabbage
3. Dinney Moore's
4. The Eureka Cafe
5. Louie Dumbrowski
6. Mother's
7. The Delmonico
8. Spinach
9. Duffy's Tavern
10. Hopalong Cassidy's cook
11. Hop Sing
12. Fat Stuff
13. William Howard Taft
14. Cheese
15. Little Lulu
16. Arthur Godfrey
17. Strawberries
18. Coconut
19. Watermelon
20. From a pear tree
21. Catsup
22. Burten Baskin and Rivine Robbins

23. Vanilla, chocolate, strawberry
24. Dagwood Bumstead
25. Crocus (flowers)
26. Wishbone
27. Corn
28. Damn yankees
29. Play-doh
30. Fanny Farmer
31. Coca-Cola
32. Nobody knows for sure. Some was found in the ancient pyramids and was still fresh enough to pop.
33. Fred Flintstone
34. Pepsi-Cola and milk
35. Pop's Soda Shop
36. Birdie
37. Cookie
38. Sargent Hacker
39. Igor
40. Lasagna
41. Lum Edwards and Abner Peabody
42. Smiley Burnett
43. Jingle Jones, played by Andy Devine
44. Humphrey Pennyworth
45. Tony Gilento
46. Jack Nicklaus
47. Sidney Greenstreet
48. Roscoe Sweeney
49. Mel Sharples
50. Rick's Cafe Americaine

Appendix

By Dr. J. Tom Cooper

I HAVE TAKEN out an appendix or two in my medical career, but this is the first time I have ever added one. Obesity is one condition that I became very familiar with early in my life. When I entered medical school in 1957, I weighed 150 pounds. Eight months later, I weighed in at 220! The problem seemed to rest in the enormous stress that medical school exerted on me.

Since my first year of medical school, I found myself going up and down like a yo-yo — dieting followed by binging, followed by another diet. This lasted for ten years. In 1967 I saw a close associate almost die from a heart attack and I took a good look at myself. I weighed 240 pounds and had abnormal blood pressure, blood sugar, cholesterol, and triglycerides. I was a coronary waiting to happen. It scared my weight off of me, and since that time I have done little else except treat obesity.

Ludlow Porch

In my career as a bariatrician (weight control doctor), I have noticed that there are a lot of physicians who mean well but just don't know how to deal with obesity. The ideal approach to treatment is to realize that there is more than a large lump of fat across the desk from me; there is a human being with feelings, a person who is trusting me to help him or her get out of the trap of being overweight.

Over the eight or so years that I have known and loved Ludlow and his family, we have discussed and shared a lot of experiences. We both agree that there is a fine line between sadness and joy, between tears and laughter, and between humor and despair. For those of us who have been exposed to a Dr. Clod, who tells you to push away from the table or who tells you that you are fat (but doesn't tell you how to deal with it), there *is* a group of doctors in this country that is willing and able to help you, or to train your doctor in the skills necessary to help you, lose those unwanted pounds.

This group is the American Society of Bariatric Physicians located in Englewood, Colorado. It has members in all fifty states, Canada, and a number of other foreign countries. You can get the addresses and names of those bariatric physicians closest to you by calling or writing the ASBP. The phone number is (303) 779-4833, and the address is 5200 South Quebec, Suite 300, Englewood, Colorado 80111.

Even with an experienced physician, it is not ever

easy to lose fat. There seems to be a number of factors necessary for success. Almost all of these have to be present, or the dieter will ultimately fail. I have listed most of these below and hope they will be of help to you.

1. Have a sense of humor. Learn to laugh and poke fun at yourself a little.

2. Be realistic. Ten pounds a week is a ridiculous goal, but I have had patients who initially expected this much and were destroyed when they could not meet this standard.

3. Be resigned to the fact that you have to either eat less, exercise more, or a combination of the two in order to consistently take off pounds.

4. Watch your environment. It's a jungle out there! Feeders and saboteurs abound. Be a little paranoid and trust nobody. There is a saying, "Just because you're paranoid, it doesn't mean that everyone's not against you."

5. Be tolerant of others while you're dieting. They have their own lives to live and can't totally change just because you're trying to lose unwanted fat.

6. Be assertive enough to let your needs be known to others without stepping on their toes too much.

7. Into your daily life let a spirit of love and forgiveness reign. This means that you permit the office or neighborhood fool to try forcing you off your diet by annoying you with a plate of brownies. The next

time, clobber him or her, preferably with an ax handle. This is known in the psychological field as "splaining" something to a person.

As a reverse psychology ploy, I give my patients a list of rules entitled "How to Fail at the Weight Loss Game." Through permission of the Weight Control Research Institute, they are printed here:

A lot of my patients want to know how to fail at losing weight. Believe me, it's easy! Just do all the things I list below or even part of them and you should have no problem keeping all of your fat deposits. Also, in the event you want to succeed, do just the OPPOSITE of what we say below.

1. Listen to all your friends when they tell you that you don't need to lose any more weight. After all, they are experts and many of them have have medical degrees, don't they? They have no reason such as jealousy or envy that would make them say something like this. Even if you're five feet tall and weigh 180 pounds, it pays to listen to fools who would sabotage your efforts to improve your health and well-being.

2. Rely on your "appetite suppressants" to do all the work for you. Ignore the massive amount of medical research that has shown that these medications are only useful as a temporary measure in con-

trolling hunger and have no long-term effect. Be sure not to build up a bunch of good habits to replace the bad habits that helped make you overweight in the first place.

3. When you go to a party or social function, be sure and starve yourself before going so that you are ravenous enough and vulnerable enough to "pig out" after you get there. In order to fail properly, be sure not to eat enough to keep you out of trouble BEFORE you leave home or work to go there.

4. Be sure to take your diuretics (water pills) more often than the directions say. Use them to take off "weight" rather than excess edema fluid. Don't worry about the potentially dangerous side effects that can occur if they are taken too often. Also, be sure to load up on forbidden foods that are high in sodium (salt), so that you can bloat up again tomorrow. Don't tell your doctor about your other medicines from other doctors, including any diuretics and heart drugs that you are taking. It would only confuse him and keep him from giving you some of the ones he uses.

5. If you make a mistake, be sure and heap a lot of guilt on yourself. A little guilt will go a long way. Once you have made that one mistake, stay off your diet the rest of the month. Be sure and deny any problems on your next visit to your doctor.

6. Become a "couch potato" and never exercise; it could become habit-forming. Do as little moving

around as possible and never take the stairs or park more than a few feet away from a store. Be sure and park in the handicapped spaces and run into the store wearing your tennis outfit or jogging suit.

7. Let your problems, anxieties, anger, sadness, or depression make you eat. It is better to crush bad feelings underneath a load of food than to deal with them in an adult manner. Get inside your shell or closet and EAT.

It is obvious to everyone that these keys to failure are not things you really should be doing. They were listed in this way to get your attention and make you think.

Take the time to sit down one day and take a good look at yourself (feet excepted). Try and realize that you are worth every bit of effort you can expend to attain your goal of health and happiness. Find yourself a *good* medical doctor with an interest in you as a person and work with him or her. Don't expect the doctor to do it all for you, but don't tolerate a Dr. Clod who wants *you* to do it all for him. Remember that obesity is probably one of the biggest causes of illness and human misery in this country.

Dr. Grant Gwinup, a famous California endocrinologist, has been quoted as saying that if we had a cure for cancer tomorrow, we could add an average of two years of life to every person in this country. He also has said that if we could somehow "cure" all obesity, we would add an additional four years of life to the same population.

It's a beautiful world out there. Take the time and make the effort to assure that your time on it is long and happy. Good luck and God bless you.

J. Tom Cooper, M.D.
October, 1984